Islamic
BANKING
SYSTEM

Islamic BANKING SYSTEM
Concepts & Applications

Sudin Haron
Bala Shanmugam

Pelanduk
Publications
www.pelanduk.com

Published by
Pelanduk Publications (M) Sdn. Bhd.
(Co. No: 113307-W)
12 Jalan SS13/3E, Subang Jaya Industrial Estate,
47500 Subang Jaya, Selangor Darul Ehsan,
Malaysia.

Address all correspondence to:
Pelanduk Publications (M) Sdn. Bhd.,
P.O. Box 8265, 46785 Kelana Jaya,
Selangor Darul Ehsan, Malaysia.

Check out our website at *www.pelanduk.com*
e-mail: *mypp@tm.net.my*

1st printing 1997
2nd printing 2001

Perpustakaan Negara Malaysia   Cataloguing-in-Publication Data

Sudin Haron
    Islamic banking system: concepts and applications /
    Sudin Haron, Bala Shanmugam
    Includes index
    ISBN 967-978-599-8
    1. Banks and banking—Islamic countries. 2. Banks and banking—
    Religious aspects—Islam. I. Bala Shanmugam. II. Title.
    297.19785

Printed by
Academe Art & Printing Services Sdn. Bhd.

Preface

Conventional banking as we know it today is the result of thousands of years of trial, error and evolution. These practices have been guided by a single albeit unwritten principle, that is, to maximise profits. Despite such simplicity and a slow evolutionary process history is replete with casualties. Islamic banking on the other hand is faced with a far greater challenge. The establishment of institutions within the spectrum of Islamic banking are in line with revelations in the Quran and teachings of Hadiths. These rules being Divine ordinance cannot, therefore, simply be amended to suit changing economic conditions and practices. In spite of such difficulties Muslim communities have been attempting for the past three decades or so, to implement a system of banking and finance which is free from interest.

Currently there are more than 150 Islamic financial institutions around the world. With the exception of Iran, Pakistan and Sudan which have completely Islamised their entire banking system, Islamic banks have gained footing in most Muslim countries. Realising the importance of this new concept of banking, various conventional banks have established their own Islamic banking departments.

Despite being established as institutions that are governed by Divine ordinance, scholars have resorted to various interpretations of these ordinance. Also each Muslim country has it own religious authorities. Consequently, the modus operandi of Islamic banking tends to vary from country to country. While the International Association of Islamic Banks is working towards standardising all aspects of Islamic banking, there nevertheless exists variations.

With the increasing popularity of Islamic banking, books in this area have become quite common. However, there has been an acute dearth of literature which tends to be more academic and covers both concepts and applications of procedures. We would like to see our book fall in this category. Furthermore, there are hardly any texts highlighting the procedural differences of existing Islamic banks. This has been one of the major impetus for the compilation of this text. The nine chapters presented herein is a comprehensive illustration of all major aspects of Islamic banking and finance. Commencing from historical times to the latest development, relevant details pertaining to Islamic banking are thoroughly discussed. This makes the book an invaluable guide to practitioners as well as persons interested in this new force in finance. Students of banking and moreso those at tertiary institutions where Islamic banking is taught will benefit from this simplified presentation of often complex concepts.

We believe that to survive in today's dynamic world of business, Islamic banks must be competitive not only within itself but also with the conventional financial system. For growth and development to occur the level of patronisation must increase. For this to occur Islamic banks must be able to outperform or must at least be on equal footings with conventional banks. With such a performance Islamic banks will be in a position to reward their patrons accordingly, thereby increasing their patronage. Herein lies a critical issue, for conventional banks have purely mercantile motives whereas Islamic banks are also bound by social motives. Being charged with social objectives often results in monetary costs. Consequently, monetary profits may not be as high as institution which work without social constraints. The question is whether Islamic banks are prepared to trade 'social motives' for 'profit motives' and if so to what extent, is something we would like our readers to contemplate upon. The authors would be pleased to hear the comments and constructive criticisms of our readers.

More than convention dictates that the authors thank our families for the support and encouragement. Finally, the authors accept responsibility for any error which is bound to exist in any topic which is subject to interpretations. We nevertheless trust that such errors would not impede serious study of the text.

Sudin Haron, UUM, Malaysia
Bala Shanmugam, UNE, Australia

Contents

vii

Tables

Figures

Chapter 1
History and Development

1.1 Introduction

In the late seventies and early eighties, Muslim communities were awoken by the emergence of Islamic banks which provided interest-free banking facilities. Pioneered by Mit Ghamr Local Savings Bank, which was established in 1963 in a provincial rural centre in the Nile Delta of Egypt, there are currently more than 150 interest-free institutions all over the world. Islamic banks nowadays not only operate in almost all Muslim countries but have also extended their wings to the Western world to serve both Muslim and non-Muslim customers.

The majority of the existing financial institutions and financial instruments that form the entire financial system available today have developed gradually. Although there is inconsistency on the exact starting period of conventional banking, scholars believe that it began in the middle of 12th century. The moneychangers and interest charges, however, have been around a lot longer. The *Sumerian* people (3,000BC-1,800BC) for example, used interest rate as the price for loans in their lending activities. Sumerian documents reveal a systematic use of credit based on loans of grain by volume and loans of metal by weight and often these loans carried interest charges (Homer, 1977).

In the case of Islamic banking, the establishment of the Mit Ghamr Local Savings Bank is said to be a milestone for modern Islamic banking. The history of Islamic banking activities can nevertheless be traced back to the birth of Islam. The second section of this chapter, will provide information about the existence of Islamic banking activities during the early years of Islam. The third section elaborates the development of modern Islamic banking system. The development of Islamic banking system in selected Muslim countries is highlighted in section four.

1.2 Islamic Banking in the Early Days of Islam

Islam was born in a city which was considered to be one of the most complex and heterogeneous places in Arabia. The Meccan community had grown beyond the limitations of clan and tribe to afford the complexity of political and economic ties (Lapidus, 1988). During this time,

1

the city prospered with business and trade with businessmen participating in loans with interest charges. Although in the early years of Islam, the task undertaken by the Prophet (*pbuh*) and his companions were to introduce Arabs to Islam, there is evidence to indicate that the development of the Islamic banking system started from the time of the Prophet (*pbuh*).

One of the most important events relating to interest was the revelations which prohibit Muslims from associating themselves with *riba* (interest). The four revelations of *Al-Quran* specifically dealing with interest are milestones which later shaped the operational aspects of the Islamic banking system. The Prophet (*pbuh*) on many occasions explained and guided Muslims in performing Islamic banking activities. For example, in one *hadith* narrated by Abu Al-Minhal, "*I asked Al-bara' bin Azib and Zaid bin 'Arqam about practising money exchange. They replied. "We are traders in the time of Allah's Apostle (pbuh) and I asked Allah's Apostle about money exchange. He replied, "If it is from hand to hand, there is no harm in it; otherwise it is not permissible.*" (Sahih Al-Bukhari, Vol.3 p.157). Beside this *hadith*, there are numerous *hadiths* relevant to banking, especially those in which the Prophet clearly prohibits Muslims from accepting or paying *riba*.

Unlike other religions where temples and clerics were heavily involved in accepting and lending money, there is no evidence to indicate that either the Prophet (*pbuh*) or the four righteous caliphs (Abu Bakr, Umar, Othman, Ali) had established or organised a financial institution with the objective of accepting deposits or making loans to Muslims. During the Sumerian civilisation for example, temples were heavily involved in lending money with interest. Similarly, during the Babylonian and Mesopotamian civilisations temples gave loans to states and individuals and accumulated much wealth (Gustave, 1926). The involvement of clerics in lending money with interest to the public continued in the early days of Christianity and prompted various Councils to issue decrees which prohibited and condemned this practice. The Canon 20 of the provincial Council of Elvira (306AD) was the first ecclesiastical legislation which prohibited usury both to the clerical and layperson. Similar prohibitions were found in the Canons issued by the Council of Arles (314AD), Council of Laodicea (325AD), Council of Nice (325AD), Council of Carthage (345AD), and the second Council of Arles (443AD)

(Divine, 1959). Although these Canons did not prohibit Christian clerics from lending money, the prohibition from accepting usury is nevertheless an evidence that Christian religious institutions were involved in banking activities.

The only known organised Islamic financial institution which originated during the time of the Prophet (*pbuh*) was called '*baitul mal*' (the exchequer of an Islamic state or public treasury). Although the mosque was used as the treasury by the Prophet (*pbuh*) it was Umar (d.644AD), the second caliph who reorganised the establishment of *baitul mal* and operated it as a separate entity (Ra'ana, 1991). The revenue for *baitul mal* came from two sources, primary and secondary. While *zakat* (alms or wealth-tax), *kharaj* (land-tax), *jazia* (poll-tax), custom duties, tolls and *sadaqah* (donations) were considered the primary sources, the secondary source comprised of property with no known owner, the property of apostates, and estates of deceased person who has no legitimate heirs. Funds collected by *baitul mal* were channelled into two broad categories of expenditure: (i) claims in regard to state responsibilities such as the expenses for the army and salaries for state officials, and (ii) to finance activities for the public benefits such as constructions of roads and water supplies (Siddiqi, 1948 and Encyclopedia of Islam, 1971).

In line with its objective of managing the financial affairs of the Islamic state, the *baitul mal* did not generally accept deposits from the public nor gave loans to those in need. There is however, evidence which indicates that *baitul mal* have extended loans to certain individuals. For example, as reported in *Muwatta* Imam Malik, Caliph Umar's sons Abd Allah and Ubayd Allah received loans from the *baitul mal* which they used, on their way back to Medina, for trading and consequently earned profits. Caliph Umar declared this transaction as *mudaraba* (profit-sharing) and requested his son to give half of the profits to *baitul mal* (Council of Islamic Ideology of Pakistan, 1983).

In the absence of state deposit taking institutions, the task of keeping other people's money and valuable items was provided by trustworthy individuals. For example, the Prophet (*pbuh*) himself was one of the individuals trusted by the people. The Prophet (*pbuh*) remained as custodian of other people's properties until his migration to Medina. Before his departure, he assigned Ali (later known as Caliph Ali i.e the fourth caliph) to return all the deposits to their rightful owners.

3

Another trustworthy individual who provided deposit facilities to the public during the early years of Islam was Az Zubair ben Al Awwam (circa 610AD). Az Zubair is said to have held deposits amounting to 2,200,000 million dirhams. He was credited as the first person who applied the Islamic principle of '*qard*' or '*loan*' in the Islamic banking system. According to Homoud (1985), Az Zubair was a person of sagacity and intelligence who preferred to accept deposits on the principle of *qard* rather than the principle of '*wadiah*' or 'trust' (see Chapter 4 for details). This move facilitated two conditions:

i.   He reserved his right to deploy the money as he saw fit.
ii. It represented a secure guarantee to the owners because the borrower is liable to return to the depositors. In the case where deposits are placed under the principle of *wadiah*, the accepter of the deposits is not liable to return the deposit if it is lost for reasons other then the negligence of the deposit taker.

Besides the concept of money exchange, prohibition of interest, and deposit under the principle of *qard*, activities related to remittance and the bill of exchange had also existed in the early days of Islam. For example, Ibn Abbas (d.686-8AD) received the *warik* (silver minted into dirhams) and sent an acknowledgment to Kufa (a city in Iraq). Similarly, Abdallah ben Az Zubair (624AD-692AD) received cash in Mecca and wrote to his brother in Iraq who repaid the depositors when they arrived in Iraq. With regard to the cheques, Sayf al-Dawalah al-Hamdani (circa 970AD) was the first person in Islamic banking history to use cheques (Homoud 1985).

The Islamic banking concept pioneered by a few activities in the early years of Islam failed to expand to become a complete banking system. The so called dark ages which swept the European Continent between the fifth to the tenth century, also had a significant impact upon Muslim countries. The revival of commercial and economic activities in European countries commencing from the twelfth century saw the emergence of the conventional banking system. This new system expanded rapidly not only in Europe but other parts of the world. Through trade activities and colonisation, this system later gained footing in Muslim countries as well.

1.3 Islamic Banking in the Modern Era

The late 19th and early 20th century is widely known as the beginning of the era of Islamic resurgence. Some of those responsible for this resurgence are as follows: Jamal al-Din al-Afghani (1838/9-1897), Muhammad Abduh (1849-1905), Rashid Rida (1865-1935), Muhammad Iqbal (1875-1938), Hassan al-Banna (1906-1949), Syyid Qutb (1906-1966), Abul Ala Mawududi (1903-1979). Their thoughts became the impetus for Muslims to apply Islamic teachings in all aspects of life including political, social and economic.

Since Islam prohibits interest in all forms and kinds, it is obvious that elimination of interest from the economic and banking system became the most popular topic among contemporary Islamic scholars. In fact the legality of interest was discussed by Abduh and *Rida* in *Al Manar*, a Cairo based magazine of the early 20th century. The discussions of the importance for Muslims to have interest-free financial institutions became intense especially in the sixties and seventies. Among the first conferences where discussions on the legality of interest was included was the second conference of the Council of Islamic Studies, University of Al Azhar, Cairo, in May 1965. In terms of scholastic contributions, persons such as Kurshid Ahmed, Muhammad Nejatullah Siddiqi, Ziauddin Ahmed, Muhammad Fahim Khan, Sami Hassan Homoud, Muhammad Abdul Manan, Muhammad Anas Zarqa, Muhammad Umar Chapra were among those who have made much contribution towards the enrichment of Islamic banking literature.

Although *fatwas* or opinions by Muslim jurists clearly stated the unlawfulness of interest dealings by conventional banks no effort was made until the early 20th century by either Muslim governments or private parties to establish Islamic banks. The first attempt to establish an interest-free bank came in Malaysia in the mid-1940s. A plan to invest prospective pilgrim savings in real estate and plantations in accordance with *Shariah* was, however, unsuccessful (Khan, S.R.1983). The first experimental local Islamic bank was established in the late 1950s in a rural area of Pakistan that charged no interest on its lending (Wilson, 1983). The establishment of Mit Ghamr Local Savings Bank marked a new milestone in the revolution of the modern Islamic banking system. This bank was considered to be the most innovative and successful experiment with interest-free banking. Located in the Nile Delta, Egypt, the Mit Ghamr Local Savings Bank provided banking services such as deposit accounts, loan accounts, equity participation, direct investment, and social services. Although these services are considered basic banking services, it was nevertheless sufficient to meet the banking needs of the surrounding community. Besides its ability to prevent customers from going to money-lenders for financial assistance, this bank was able to instil a sense of belonging among its customers. These were the contributing factors towards its success. One of the most important contributions made by this bank to Islamic banking history was that it proved to the Muslim community that there was an alternative to the conventional banking system. However, the turbulent political situation adversely affected the bank. Its operations were consequently undertaken by the National Bank of Egypt and the Central Bank in the second half of 1967. As a result of this action, the interest-free concept was abandoned and Mit Ghamr's operations, reverted to an interest-based system. In 1971, under the regime of Mr. Sadat, the interest-free concept was revived and a new institution by the name of Nasser Social Bank was established to carry out businesses based on *Shariah* concepts.

Although Mit Ghamr had to cease operations before reaching a maturity period and before it was able to extend services to all business sectors, it nevertheless signalled to the Muslim community that Islamic principles were still applicable to modern day business. This phenomenon awoke Muslim scholars around the world. These scholars started studying and examining the operations of this pioneering bank. Scarcity of literature and the non-existence of a complete set of *Shariah* law guidelines often hampered their effort. These set-backs, however, were not viewed as stumbling blocks for those who wanted to go back to religion. Moved by the resurgence of Islam, Muslim scholars continued their struggle in expediting the establishment of Islamic bank in their respective countries. Realising the scarcity and unavailability of resources, the first task to be carried out was to formulate the theoretical frameworks and guidelines on practical aspects of Islamic banking. The task to formulate frameworks and guidelines were obviously vested in the hands of Muslim theologians and economists. Getting Muslim economists who possessed detailed knowledge in *Shariah* laws was indeed a difficult job. In many instances, those who possessed knowledge in Islamic laws were non-economist and vice-versa. To complicate the matter further, most Muslim economists were educated in Western economics and did not have sufficient knowledge in Islamic economics. In Pakistan for example, out of the nineteen members of the Council of Islamic Ideology, i.e. the first body set-up by General Zia whose task was to develop a framework for the elimination of interest from the economy, only one member could be labelled as an expert in this field. Eleven of them received education from *Madrasa* (Religious schools) (Gieraths, 1990). These initial difficulties, however, were overcome especially where the government also played a supportive role in promoting the ideas of establishing an Islamic bank.

The initial step in establishing the Islamic bank in various countries has largely been undertaken by private initiatives. The late King Faisal bin Abdul Aziz Al-Saud of Saudi Arabia, was one of the noteworthy individuals who had made a major contribution toward Islamic economics by initiating the establishment of the Organisation of Islamic Conferences (OIC). Under His Majesty's leadership and initiative, Muslim countries were urged to establish Islamic financial and economic institutions which were free from *riba* (interest) (Ali, 1988).

The second conference of OIC of Foreign Ministers which was held in Karachi, Pakistan in December 1970, passed a resolution that a study be made on the establishment of an International Islamic Bank for Trade and Development together with a Federation of Islamic Banks. The task of preparing the proposal of these institutions was given to experts from 18 Islamic countries. In presenting their report, the experts recommended the establishment of three institutions. The first institution was the International Islamic Bank whose function is very similar to the normal commercial bank; second was the Investment and Development Body of Islamic Countries which functions as an investment institution and finally the Association of Islamic Banks which serves as a consultative body in the field of Islamic economy and banking. The experts also recommended that the institutions to be established must be based on a profit-and-loss sharing participation arrangement.

Foreign Ministers of Islamic countries met again in Bengazi, Libya in March, 1973. During this meeting, the Ministers examined the proposal of the establishment of the various institutions as suggested in the earlier report. It was decided that a financial and economic department should be set up within the Islamic Secretariat. In July, 1973 a committee of experts from oil-producing Islamic countries met in Jeddah and discussed the establishment of an Islamic bank. Their subsequent meeting was held in May, 1974 where the bank's charter, its rules and regulations were drafted. This draft was approved in August 1974 by the Finance Ministers of OIC. The Islamic Development Bank (IDB) was officially established in October 1975 with a founding member of 22 Islamic countries. The Bank's principal office is located in Jeddah, Saudi Arabia and has two regional offices in Rabat, Morocco and in Kuala Lumpur, Malaysia. At the end of 1994, the bank had 47 member countries. In addition to the financial assistance for the development purposes provided for member countries, the bank also extended its assistance to member countries who wanted to establish Islamic banks in their own countries. IDB also plays an important role in conducting and promoting research especially in the area of Islamic economics, banking and finance.

Specifically, the functions of IDB as stated in its 1994's annual report are as follows:

> "The functions of the Bank are to participate in equity capital and grant loans for productive projects and enterprises besides providing financial assistance to member countries in other forms for economic and social development. The Bank is also required to establish and operate special funds for specific purposes including a fund for assistance to Muslim communities in non-member countries, in addition to setting up trust funds.
>
> The Bank is authorised to accept deposits and to mobilise financial resources by way of appropriate modes of financing. It is also charged with the responsibility of assisting in the promotion of foreign trade, especially in capital goods, among member countries, providing technical assistance to member countries, extending training facilities for personnel engaged in development activities in Muslim countries to conform to the *Shariah*."

The establishment of the Islamic Development Bank in 1975 paved the way for the establishment of other Islamic banks in various Muslim countries. Immediately after the establishment of the Islamic Development Bank in 1975, The Dubai Islamic Bank was incorporated. In the year 1977, three more Islamic banks commenced business i.e. Faisal Islamic Bank of Egypt, Faisal Islamic Bank of Sudan, and Kuwait Finance

8

House. The Islamic banks which were incorporated in the late 1970s and early 1980s are shown in Table 1.1.

Table 1.1
List of Islamic Banks

Name	Country	Date of Establishment
Nasser Social Bank	Egypt	1972
Islamic Development Bank	Saudi Arabia	1975
Dubai Islamic Bank	United Arab Emirate	1975
Faisal Islamic Bank of Egypt	Egypt '	1977
Faisal Islamic Bank of Sudan	Sudan	1977
Kuwait Finance House	Kuwait	1977
Islamic Banking System International Holding	Luxembourg	1978
Jordan Islamic Bank	Jordan	1978
Bahrain Islamic Bank	Bahrain	1979
Dar al-Mal al-Islami	Switzerland	1981
Bahrain Islamic Inv. Company	Bahrain	1981
Islamic International Bank for Investment & Development	Egypt	1981
Islamic Investment House	Jordan	1981
Al-Baraka Investment and Development company	Saudi Arabia	1982
Saudi-Philippine Islamic Development Bank	Saudi Arabia	1982
Faisal Islamic Bank Kibris	Turkey	1982
Bank Islam Malaysia Berhad	Malaysia	1983
Islami Bank Bangladesh Ltd	Bangladesh	1983
Islamic Bank International	Denmark	1983
Tadamon Islamic Bank	Sudan	1983
Qatar Islamic Bank	Qatar	1983
Beit Ettamouil Saudi Tounsi	Tunisia	1984
West Sudan Islamic Bank	Sudan	1985
Albaraka Turkish Finance Hse	Turkey	1985
Faisal Finance Institution	Turkey	1985
Al Rajhi Company for Currency Exchange & Commerce	Saudi Arabia	1985
Al-Ameen Islamic & Financial Investment Corp. India Ltd.	India	1985

Although the ideas to establish the Islamic bank had been discussed in Islamic countries since 1970, the process of establishing Islamic banks in individual countries varied from one country to another. Iran, Pakistan and Sudan, for example, converted their entire financial system to an interest-free system. In other countries, however, Islamic banks supplemented interest-based banks. In Malaysia, Egypt and Saudi Arabia, conventional banks are allowed to offer banking services based on Islamic principles. This method is commonly known as 'Islamic windows'.

Currently, it is estimated that the worldwide assets of the Islamic banking system exceed US$60 billion. A study of the experiences of Iran and Pakistan shows that the adoption of Islamic banking has not led to the collapse of the financial system as some had feared. There has been rapid growth of private sector deposits in Islamic modes in both nations, demonstrating that the system can be effective in mobilising resources (Khan and Mirakhor, 1990). The commitment of government also plays an important role in assisting the development of the Islamic financial system. In Malaysia, for example, the government has given its full support to the development of an interest-free financial system functioning side-by-side with the conventional system. By the beginning of 1993, a total of 21 Islamic banking products were successfully developed by the Central Bank of Malaysia and at the end of December 1993 a total of 21 financial institutions participated in the interest-free banking scheme. Another breakthrough in the Islamic banking system in Malaysia was the implementation of Islamic inter-bank money market which began on January 3, 1994. This market covers three aspects, namely, the inter-bank trading in Islamic financial instruments; Islamic inter-bank investments; and the Islamic inter-bank cheque clearing system.

Another organisation which served as an impetus for the establishment and promotion of Islamic banking is The International Association of Islamic Banks. This organisation was established on 20th August 1977 under the auspices of the OIC in Jeddah, Saudi Arabia. Currently there are 35 Islamic banks which have subscribed as full members. While the head office of the Association is located in Jeddah, the regional offices are in Karachi and London. This Association does not provide any financial assistance but assists in enhancing cooperation among its members. The objectives of the Association are as follows (IAIB, 1994):

i. Promoting the philosophy and principles of Islamic Banking.
ii. Pursuing the objectives of establishing operational standards for Islamic financial institutions.
iii. Establishing parameters for cooperation and coordination amongst the institutions.
iv. Providing assistance in manpower development.
v. Promoting the institution of new Islamic banks and assisting them in all conceivable aspects.
vi. Representing, mediating and acting as arbitrator for and among Islamic banks.
vii. Maintaining a database for all Islamic financial institutions.
viii. Developing an inter-Islamic banks market to encourage the flow of funds amongst Islamic banks.

1.4 Developments of Islamic banking in Selected Muslim Countries

News about the existence and achievements made by the Mit Ghamr Savings Bank in Egypt and the establishment of the Islamic Development ment Bank reached Muslim scholars and jurists throughout the Muslim world. These scholars consequently took steps to establish Islamic banks in their own countries, often with the support of the respective governments. The approach and commitment of various Muslim governments varied from country to country. This section will highlight the development of Islamic banking in selected Muslim countries. The selected countries include Egypt, Iran, Malaysia, Pakistan, Sudan and Turkey.

1.4.1 Egypt

As mentioned earlier the establishment of Mit Ghamr Local Savings Bank in the Nile Delta is considered one of the most important events in the history of Islamic banking. The introduction of banking services based on Islamic principles by this bank received overwhelming support from customers. The number of depositors increased tremendously from 17,560 in their first financial year (1963/1964) to 251,152 in the financial year ending 1966/1967. The amount of deposits also increased from LE 40,944 at the end of the first financial year to LE 1,828,375 at the end of 1966/1967 year. The Ford Foundation in its 1967 Annual Report praised the success of Mit Ghamr in winning support from farmers and villagers (El Askher, 1990). Due to the changes in the political atmosphere in Egypt, the operations of Mit Ghamr were undertaken by the National Bank of Egypt and subsequently the interest-free products and services were abandoned.

The introduction of interest in the operations of Mit Ghamr had reduced the number of depositors substantially. The new regime of Anwar Sadat revitalised the interest-free banking concept and in 1971 a new bank called Nasser Social Bank was established. Unlike Mit Ghamr where the setting-up was under private initiative, Nasser Social Bank was a government owned bank. Since then, three more Islamic banks, Faisal Islamic Bank of Egypt, Islamic International Bank for Investment and Development, and Egyptian Saudi Finance Bank have been granted licences to operate in Egypt.

Among these banks, the Faisal Islamic Bank of Egypt is the only bank which received special privileges from the government. It was established by a special act called Law No 48/1977 on the Establishment of Faisal Islamic Bank of Egypt and Decree No 77 (1977) of the Ministry of Wakf which enacted the statutes of the Faisal Islamic Bank of Egypt. This bank was established as an Egyptian Joint Stock Company and the Article 10 of Law No 48/1977 states that:

"The laws governing foreign exchange operations, public institutions and organisations or those of a public benefit nature as well as public sector companies shall not apply to the Bank and its branches.

Similarly, the provision of joint stock Companies law shall not apply to the bank in so far as a special provision is provided for in this law.

The bank shall be subject to the laws on the control of banks and credit as concerns its operations in local currency always without prejudice to the provisions of this law."

Similarly, Article 14 stipulates:

"The laws and regulations concerning labour and employment, wages and salaries, remunerations, pensions, medical treatment and social insurances, whether those applicable to Government, public institutions and organisations, public sector companies or joint stock companies, as well as rules governing the travel of employees, shall not apply to the Chairman and members of the Board of Directors of the Bank and all its employees and institutions. The Board of Directors of the Bank shall issue an internal regulation covering the entire affairs of the Chairman and members of the Board of Directors of the Bank and its employees comprising the organisation of all matters related to their functions, provided same shall not be less than the minimum stipulated by the law for the private sector."

The above clauses conferred Faisal Islamic Bank of Egypt a special status and facilitated its operations. Except for Nasser Social Bank, where some banking facilities are not available due to certain restrictions imposed by the authority, other Islamic banks offer similar banking facilities to those available at conventional banks. Deposit facilities such as current accounts, savings accounts, and investment (term deposits) accounts are available at these Islamic banks. In terms of financing, both short term and long term financing are provided by the banks based on *Shariah* principles. Like other banks, Islamic banks in Egypt are supervised by the central bank. Islamic banks have to observe both statutory and liquidity reserve requirements. In terms of performance, a recent study found that conventional banks out performed Islamic banks (Saeed, 1995). Like Islamic banks elsewhere, Islamic banks in Egypt have limited investment opportunities. Also Islamic securities are not issued by the government. Another recent development in the Egyptian Islamic banking system is the establishment of Islamic Transaction branches by the Bank of Egypt. These branches provide banking facilities based on *Shariah* principles similar to those facilities available at Islamic banks. The Bank of Egypt, however, is not an Islamic bank.

1.4.2 Islamic Republic of Iran

The history of the Iranian Islamic banking system started immediately after the Islamic revolution which ousted the Shah's regime in 1979. The implementation of Islamic banking, however was on a gradual basis and took six years to be fully implemented. Subsequent to the Revolution, there were about 35 banks in Iran and the system relied on both the government and the private sectors, as well as the domestic and foreign sectors for funds (Pourian, 1993). During the turmoil of the revolution, the banking system faced various problems such as flight of capital and 'run' on banks. On June 8, 1979, the banking system was nationalised by the Revolutionary Council. There was also a reduction in the number of banks through amalgamation. As a result of this amalgamation, the banking system was only represented by six commercial banks and three specialised banks. In addition, 22 provincial banks (one for each province) were established (Hedayati, 1993).

The first step taken by the new regime towards the establishment of an Islamic banking system in Iran was the introduction of a 'maximum service charge' and a 'guaranteed minimum profit' into the banking system. At the same time, a comprehensive legislation to bring the operations of the entire banking system into total compliance with *Shariah* was prepared by a group of individuals from various backgrounds. The proposed legislation was submitted to the Revolutionary Council in March 1982 and was passed by the Parliament in August 1983 as the 'Law for Usury-Free Banking'. This law is broadly divided into five topics namely, 'Objectives and duties of banking system', 'The mobilisation of monetary resources', 'Banking facilities', 'The Central Bank and the monetary policy', and 'Miscellaneous'. Subsequently, there were four more notes approved by the Parliament and these notes were considered as part of Usury-Free law. These notes comprise of 'Regulations relating to the Law for Usury-Free Banking', 'Regulations relating to the granting of banking facilities', 'Regulations relating to Chapter 4 of the Law for Usury-Free Banking', and 'Regulations relating to Chapter 5 of the Law for Usury-Free banking'. This new law was implemented on March 21, 1984.

This new law required banks to convert their outstanding interest-based to interest-free deposits within a one year period. The banks were also required to convert their entire operations as outlined by the new law within three years from the date when this law was approved by Parliament. Commencing from March 21, 1984, no bank was allowed to provide interest-based deposit or credit facilities. From March, 1985 all banking transactions were strictly based on *Shariah* (Aryan, 1990).

The law specified that the banks were allowed to accept two types of deposits, *Gharz-al-hasaned* (widely known as *qard hassan*) and investment term deposits. Both current and savings accounts fall within the *gharz-al-hasaned* deposit category. While current and savings deposits are considered as a part of a bank's resources and returns to the depositors are at the discretion of the banks, investment deposits are treated as depositor's resources. The law also states that funds in investment accounts be mobilised via the following interest-free means: joint venture, *mozarabeh* (or *mudaraba*), hire-purchase, instalment transaction, *mozaraah*, *mosaqat*, direct investment, forward dealings and *joalah* transactions (details in Chapter 4 and 6).

A study on the achievements made by the new system indicates that there has been a rapid growth of private sector deposits, demonstrating that the system can be effective in mobilising resources (Khan and Mirakhor, 1990). Like Islamic banks in other countries, instead of participating in profit-sharing activities, banks in Iran are channelling most of their funds towards mark-up activities (the difference between these activities is highlighted in Chapter 4). For example, total funds in instalment sales financing of all Iranian banks were 33.3 per cent as at 1985 and increased to 46.7 per cent at the end of 1992. On the contrary, during the corresponding period, funds channelled through *mudaraba* decreased from 18.1 per cent to 9.6 per cent (Pourian, 1993).

After more than a decade of the Islamisation of the banking system, there is evidence which indicates the existence of interest in lending activities in Iran. For example, practices of lending with interest to individuals and small-medium businesses are prevalent at uncontrolled money markets at the bazaar (Nomani and Rahnema, 1994). Similarly, the government continues to borrow from banks on the basis of a fixed rate of return. According to *Shi'a* Sect, transactions between and among the elements of the public sector, including Bank Markazi (the central bank of Iran) and commercial banks that are wholly nationalised, can take place on the basis of a fixed rate of return. The fixed rate is not viewed as interest by *Shi'a's* teachings (Iqbal and Mirakhor, 1987). In the case of international banking, the transactions and dealing with foreign banks, correspondents, and agents are still based on interest and the Iranian government has yet to revolve this issue (Ahmad, 1994).

Another financial institution in Iran which offers banking facilities but which is beyond the supervision of the central bank is the Islamic Economic Organisation (IEQ). This institution was originally an Islamic bank and was established immediately after the revolution to undertake interest-free banking activities. Following the directive of the late Imam Khomeini, this institution was excluded from nationalisation. Being independent from central bank supervision, this institution has its own policy and in most cases is not tailored to the monetary policy of the government. At present IEQ controls more than two per cent of the private sector's liquidity. In order to increase its capital base, this organisation is expanding its activities to cover trade, construction, imports and exports (Nomani and Rahnema, 1994).

1.4.3 Malaysia

The Islamic banking system in Malaysia is considered to be more progressive compared to the systems in other Muslim countries. Its history began when Bank Islam Malaysia Berhad (BIMB) was established in 1983 and now this system is complemented by the Islamic financial market, Islamic windows, and the Islamic stock market. The Malaysian Islamic banking system served as a model for Islamic banks in Indonesia and Brunei.

Like any other Muslim country, the move towards establishing an Islamic bank in Malaysia was initiated by private parties. The first formal request was made during the Bumiputera Economic Congress in 1980. This Congress passed a resolution which required the government to allow the Pilgrimage Board to establish an Islamic bank. In another seminar which was held in 1981 at the National University of Malaysia, the participants requested the government to promulgate special law which would allow the setting up of a new bank based on Islamic principles. In line with these requests, the government, on July 30, 1981 appointed a National Steering Committee on Islamic Banking, chaired by Raja Mohar Raja Badiozaman, the then economic adviser to the Prime Minister of Malaysia. The secretarial functions were given to the Pilgrimage Board of Malaysia. This committee studied both the operations of the Faisal Islamic Bank of Egypt and the Faisal Islamic Bank of Sudan (Connors, 1988). Below are among the recommendations made by the committee in its report which was presented to the Prime Minister of Malaysia on July 5, 1982 (BIMB, 1984):

1. The government should establish an Islamic bank whose operations are in accordance to the principles of *Shariah*.
2. The proposed bank is to be incorporated as a company under the auspices of the Companies Act, 1965.
3. Since the Banking Act of 1973 is not applicable for the operations of an Islamic bank, a new Islamic banking act must be introduced to license and supervise the Islamic bank. The super-

vision and administration of the proposed act are to be the responsibility of the Central Bank of Malaysia.

4. The Islamic bank is to establish its own *Shariah* Supervisory Board whose function is to ensure that the operations of Islamic bank are in accordance to the *Shariah*.

The Islamic Banking Act, 1983 which was gazetted on March 10, 1983 and came into effect on April 7, 1983 paved the way for the establishment of Islamic banking in Malaysia. This Act provides the Central Bank of Malaysia with powers to supervise and regulate Islamic banks in Malaysia. Simultaneously, the government introduced the Government Investment Act in 1983 to enable the government to issue Government Investment Certificates, which are government bonds issued in accordance to Islamic principles.

The first Islamic bank, Bank Islam Malaysia Berhad (BIMB) was incorporated on March 1, 1983 and commenced operations on July 1, of the same year. The bank now has a network of more than 50 branches. BIMB is not only promoting Islamic banking products through its own operations but is actively involved in introducing Islamic financial products and services through its own subsidiaries. At present, BIMB has subsidiaries dealing with leasing businesses, nominee services, family and general *takaful* (insurance) business, trust funds, and stockbroking.

The establishment of BIMB marked the beginning of a commitment by the Malaysian government to introduce Islamic banking in Malaysia. The present government however does not have any intention of Islamisation of the entire financial system. On the contrary, it was the long-term objective of the Central Bank of Malaysia to create an Islamic banking system parallel to the conventional system. The Central bank believes that this objective can be accomplished through: (i) a large number of players, (ii) a broad variety of instruments, and (iii) an Islamic inter-bank market (Bank Negara Malaysia, 1994).

In the process of increasing the number of players in the system, rather than allowing a new Islamic bank to operate, the Central Bank has introduced a scheme known as 'Skim Perbankan Tanpa Faedah' or the 'Interest-Free Banking Scheme'. Under this scheme often known as 'Islamic windows', all commercial banks, merchant banks and finance companies are given an opportunity to introduce Islamic banking products and services. The pilot phase of this scheme was launched on March 4, 1993 which involved the three largest commercial banks in Malaysia. The second phase started on August 21, 1993 with 10 more financial institutions joining the scheme. At the end of December 1993, a total number of 21 financial institutions had obtained the Central Bank's approval to participate in the scheme.

The Central Bank of Malaysia is also actively involved in formulating and establishing banking products whose operations do not violate *Shariah* principles. By the beginning of 1993, a total of 21 Islamic banking products were successfully developed by the Central Bank. These products represent the common products and services available at conventional banks except that they followed Shariah principles. In January, 1994 the Islamic inter-bank market was introduced in the Malaysian financial system. This market consists of three elements namely, (i) interbank trading in financial instruments, (ii) Islamic inter-bank investments, and (iii) Islamic inter-bank cheque clearing system.

1.4.4 Pakistan

Like Iran, Islamisation of the banking system in Pakistan took place at the end of 1970's. The intention to introduce this system, however, can be traced back as far as forty years ago. Mohammed Ali Jinnah, the Father of the Nation on the occasion of the opening of the State Bank of Pakistan on July, 1948 announced the Islamisation of the Pakistani banking system. The Islamisation of the economy, was again reaffirmed in the Objectives Resolution passed by the Constituent Assembly of Pakistan in 1949 (Mirakhor, 1990). However, like in other Muslim countries, the structural inflexibility and colonial mentality might be the factors which caused delays in the implementation of the pronounced objectives.

The revolutionary measure of converting the financial system towards *Shariah* laws began as a result of General Zia's *coup d'etat* in 1977. In September 1977, a Council of Islamic Ideology (CII) comprising of 19 members, was set-up by the General with the task of developing a framework for the elimination of *riba* in the economy. Since the majority of the members were non-economist, the Council appointed a 15 member panel of economists and bankers to assist them in preparing a report for the General. Subsequently, based on the report prepared by the panel of economists and bankers, CII presented its own report to General Zia on June 15 1980. Besides this Committee, there were other groups formed by other bodies to study the process of elimination of interest in the Pakistani banking system. For example, the State Bank of Pakistan in April 1979, formed six working groups to examine and make recommendations for the elimination of interest from various sectors in the economy. Similarly the Pakistan Banking Council also formed a 'Superior Task Force' which was responsible to device the necessary procedures for the implementation of an interest free banking (Siddiqi, 1985). Among these groups, only the works of the CII has been widely publicised in Islamic banking literature.

The comprehensive report presented by the CII to President Zia covered the following five topics:

i. Issues, problems and strategy.
ii. Commercial banking.
iii. Specialised financial institutions.
iv. Central banking and monetary policy.
v. Government transactions.

A number of possible devices which can be used to replace the fixed interest system was recommended by the Council. The recommended devices included the following: service charge, indexation of bank deposit and advances, leasing, investment auctioning, *bai muajjal* (deferred payment sale), hire purchase, financing on the basis of normal rate of return, time multiple counter-loans, and special loan facilities. The expected date for the implementation of interest-free system was also announced in the Report.

The second section of the Report elaborated the operations of commercial banks in an interest-free system. The recommendations included various operative aspects in financing, deposit taking and other miscellaneous transactions. An important discussion here, was the calculation of profit and loss between the bank and the borrower. The Council also suggested that the fixed return on savings and time deposits be replaced by a variable return based on profit-sharing concept. Miscellaneous transactions highlighted by the Council included inter-bank transactions, financial assistance from the State Bank, foreign transactions of banks involving interest and bank's loans to their employees.

Inter-bank transactions including those with the State Bank were recommended to be undertaken on a profit-sharing basis. Interest free loans were suggested to be given to employees of banks. No concrete solution was given by the Council with regards to foreign interest-based transactions. Pending an appropriate solution agreeable by *Shariah*, the Council suggested that a separate corporation should be established to administer foreign branches of all Pakistani banks. Foreign currency deposits held by Pakistani banks were to be transfered to this corporation and the proposed corporation was to be prohibited from accepting local deposits.

The specialised financial institutions included in the Council report were the Pakistan Industrial Credit and Investment Corporation, Industrial Development Bank of Pakistan, National Development Finance Corporation, Agricultural Development Bank of Pakistan, Small Business Finance Corporation, Equity Participation Fund, Federal Bank for Co-operatives and other co-operative credit institutions, and insurance companies. Suggestions were made on how these institutions could Islamise their operations.

The Council believed that the responsibilities and functions of the State Bank of Pakistan (the central bank) under the interest-free system should remain unchanged. It would continue to perform all functions of a modern central bank including the issue of currency, regulating of money and credit, be banker and adviser to the Government, and be the ultimate reservoir of liquidity for the financial and banking system. The monetary policy instruments suggested by the Council included minimum cash reserve requirement, liquidity ratio requirement, overall ceilings on the lending and investment operations of banks, mandatory targets for providing finance for priority sectors, selective credit controls, issue of directives to banks on various aspects of banking operations not covered by specific policy instruments, and moral suasion.

Matters relating to government transactions were also discussed by the Council Report. The Council suggested that loans involving government bodies (e.g. loans from the State Bank to the Government, or loans by Federal Government to the Provincial Government) be conducted on an interest-free basis. In the case of external borrowing which involved interest, the Council admitted that the practice will have to be continued on the basis of interest, but simultaneously advised the gov-

ernment to make an effort to reduce involvement in interest-based foreign loans.

The introduction of the interest-free system in Pakistan, however,
was not concurrent with the CII report. In fact it started much earlier. In
1979, four financial institutions, namely, House Building Finance Corporation, Investment Corporation of Pakistan, National Investment Trust
and Bankers Equity Limited started offering facilities based on *Shariah*
principles. In early June 1980, the State Bank of Pakistan started using
'profit-sharing' and 'mark-up' methods for transactions involving provincial and central government bodies, and also with certain govern-
ment-owned enterprises. In the same year, the '*Modaraba Companies
and Modaraba Ordinance*' was announced. By January, 1981 all banks
had a counter for accounts based on profit-sharing and since then many
more financial services based on *Shariah* have been introduced. Prior to
1985, banks in Pakistan were still allowed to offer interest-based product. However, the Finance Minister on June 15 1984, in his budget
speech announced that interest-based transactions were to cease in six
months. From January, 1985 all financial transactions which involved
government, state enterprises and stock companies became interest-free.
A similar rule applied to all other entities effective April of the same
year. As of July 15 1985 all deposits placed with the financial institutions became interest-free. (Gieraths, 1990).

Unlike Iran and other Muslim countries which promulgated special
laws to govern the operations of Islamic banks in their countries, except
for the '*Modaraba Companies and Modaraba (Floatation and Control)
Ordinance, 1980*' no other special laws were initially passed by the
Pakistan Government to deal with the Islamisation of the banking system. Most of the directions were given by the State Bank of Pakistan in
the form of circulars. Some examples of circulars issued by the State
Bank of Pakistan which were related to the Islamisation process are
given in Table 1.2.

Table 1.2
Circulars Related to the Islamisation Process in Pakistan

Date & No of Circulars	Contents
Circular No. 13, June 20 1984	1. Program of elimination of riba from the system. 2. Permissible modes of financing.

	3. Permissible modes of financing for various transactions.
Circular No 26, Nov. 26 1984	Rate of service charge recoverable on finances provided by way of lending other than '*qard-e-hasana*'.
Circular No. 34, Nov. 26 1984	Determination of rates of profit on various types of PLS liabilities of the banks and development finance institutions.
Circular No. 37, Dec. 10 1984	Rates of profit in case of trade-related modes of financing.
Circular No. 38, Dec. 10 1984	Rates of profit in the case of investment type modes of financing

Subsequently a new law was promulgated by the Pakistani Government known as the 'Banking Tribunal Ordinance, 1984'. The purpose of this law was to safeguard the interest of banks against delays and defaults in repayment by customers. The Tribunal established under this Ordinance is required to hear and decide any case within ninety days of the filing of the complaint. Parties involved in the dispute are allowed to appeal against the verdict given by the Tribunal to the High Court of Appeal. The Tribunal can also impose fines where parties fail to observe the decision within thirty days (Ahmad, 1994).

The Islamisation process in Pakistan is said to be far from complete. In the case of public borrowings, for example, the government is still paying interest on national and international debts (Nomani and Rahnema, 1994). Also all banks prefer to use trade related mode of financing rather than profit-loss sharing. Another serious deficiency is that there is no institutional mechanism responsible to scrutinise and validate the operating procedures of banks and other financial institutions from the *Shariah* point of view. Recently the Federal *Shariah* Court in one of its judgements ruled that financing based on mark-up practised by banks is not in conformity with the injunction of Islam (Ahmad, 1994).

1.4.5 Sudan

Sudan is the third Muslim country which has Islamised its entire banking system. The Islamic banking system, however, started in Sudan in 1977 when the Faisal Islamic Bank of Sudan (FIBS) was established. During this time, the Government of Sudan was very receptive to the establishment of Islamic banks and FIBS was established under a special law known as the 'FIBS Act of the National People's Council'. The success of FIBS encouraged authorities to allow the establishment of other Islamic banks. Subsequently, five more Islamic banks were established namely, Tadamon Islamic Bank, the Sudanese Islamic Bank, the Islamic Co-operative Bank, Al Baraka Bank of Sudan and Islamic Bank for Western Sudan.

In September 1983, the Government of Sudan made the first attempt to Islamise the entire banking system. All banks were asked to change their activities according to *Shariah*. By September 1984, the entire banking system was supposed to operate in accordance to Islamic principles. In practice, however, conventional banks continued with the interest-based system. The conversion appeared only in ledgers submitted to the Central Bank of Sudan. The resistance to this Islamisation process not only came from the conventional banks but also from policymakers who were discontented with the procedures involved in the conversion process. They believed that this conversion was merely a political gimmick (Ahmed, 1990).

The Islamic banking system in Sudan faced a major set-back when the government which wished to Islamise the entire banking system was overthrown in 1985. Consequently, all Islamic banks which were previously enjoying various privileges faced stiff regulation from the Central Bank. All concessions awarded by the previous regime were withdrawn. Except for Islamic banks which continue their operations in accordance to *Shariah*, all commercial banks have ceased to offer Islamic modes of operations and interest-based products were revitalised. The Islamic banking system again received special attention in 1994 when the existing government decided to re-Islamise the entire banking system. This time it was reported that the transformation process was done in a more earnest and a much more organised manner (Ahmad, 1994).

1.4.6 Turkey

The history and development of Islamic banking system in Turkey deserves special recognition. This is because Turkey is the only Muslim country which chose to follow a path of complete secularism. Nowhere in its Constitution is the word Islam mentioned despite the fact that 99 per cent of population are Muslims. Article 24 of the Constitution makes clear that religion must be kept separate from other matters. In fact no one is allowed to exploit or abuse religion for the purpose of personal or political gains.

The move towards the establishment of Islamic bank in Turkey began in 1983. Prior to the general election, the prime minister pledged to the electorate that the government would promulgate a specific legislation to allow the establishment of an Islamic bank in Turkey. Although this pledge was seem only as an election promise, it appeared that Turkey had been pressured by certain member states within the Organisation of Islamic Countries and the Islamic Development Bank to open its doors to the Islamic banks (Baldwin, 1990).

Immediately after the election, the Council of Ministers decreed a special law, Decree 83/7506 on December 16, 1983 which paved the way for the establishment of Islamic banks in Turkey. This law contains 17 articles and describes the methods and procedures of the founding of the Special Finance Houses and their activities. Besides this law, there were other laws and regulations issued by related parties concerning Islamic banking in Turkey. For example, comprehensive rules and regulations were issued by the Undersecretariat of the Treasury and Foreign Trade. This law was published in the Official Gazette on February 25, 1984 and covers various aspects such as the establishment, operating structures, types of funds acceptable by the institutions, the services institutions may offer, the liquidation of institutions and legal proceedings related to Islamic banking.

Another law related to the Islamic banks in Turkey was issued by the Central Bank of Turkey. This law was published in the Official Gazette on March 21, 1984. Its contains 18 articles and covers the following topics: (i) regulations concerning licence, (ii) regulations concerning permission for commencement of operations, (iii) provisions regarding the utilisation of foreign currency accumulated in the accounts, and (iv) general provision.

One of the most interesting features of all the laws relating to Islamic banks in Turkey is that words such as 'Islam' or 'Shariah' are non-existent. It is believed that the use of 'Special Finance House' instead of 'Islamic Bank' was an attempt by the authorities to avoid an open conflict with the aims and principles contained in the secular constitution (Baldwin, 1990).

24

Without including the Faisal Islamic Bank of Kibris which operates in the Turkish Republic of Northern Cyprus, there are two Islamic banks in Turkey, Albaraka Turkish Finance House and Faisal Finance Institution Incorporation. Both banks provide deposits and financing facilities. Deposit facilities are in the form of current accounts and profit-loss sharing accounts. Accounts can be opened in Turkish Lira or in foreign currencies. Financing facilities are given in the form of production support operations (*murabaha*), profit and loss partnership (*musharaka* or *mudaraba*), leasing (*ijara*) and lease purchase (*ijara wa-iktina*). Other banking services such as remittances, letters of credit, letters of guarantee, and foreign exchange transactions are also available.

1.5 Summary

The history of Islamic banking began from the early days of Islam. The most important event which later shaped the practices of banking in Islam were the revelations which prohibited Muslims from dealing with *riba*. In addition to these revelations, the prophet (*pbuh*) on many occasions condemned the 'taker and giver' of *riba*. There is also evidence that today's banking activities such as money-exchange businesses, remittance services and the usage of cheques have been in existence during the early Islamic civilisation. Nevertheless, an organised Islamic financial institution was not established during the pioneering years of Islam. The functions of financial institutions, however, were undertaken by individuals. Unlike conventional banking which developed simultaneously with the revival of commercial activities in the European continent from the thirteenth century, Islamic banking activities failed to expand. Through trade activities and colonialism, Muslim countries began to adopt conventional banking and Islamic banking activities which were initiated by early Muslims, ceased to exist.

The "so-called" Islamic resurgence which swept many parts of the Muslim worlds was the renewal point of Islamic banking system. The main notion of these resurgences was the application of Islamic teachings in all aspects of life. Since Islam prohibits interest, it is obvious that the elimination of interest from the economic and banking system became top prioritiy among Muslim scholars. The establishment of Mit Ghamr Local Savings Bank in 1963 marked a new milestone in the revolution of the modern Islamic banking system. There are currently more than 150 interest-free institutions all over the world. These institutions not only operate in almost all Muslim countries but have also extended their operations to Western countries and serve both Muslim and non-Muslim customers. Islamic banks are now in a position of offering almost all basic banking facilities to their customers.

Except for Iran, Pakistan and Sudan where the entire banking system is interest-free, dual-banking systems are maintained in other Muslim countries. In some countries such as Malaysia, Egypt and Saudi Arabia, conventional banks are permitted to offer banking services based on Islamic principles. Despite more that 10 years of experience, the Islamic banking system is said to be far from comprehensive. In Iran, for example, international banking is still interest based and the government still borrows from banks on a fixed rate of return. Similarly, the Pakistani government is continuing to deal in interest transactions. One problem faced by Islamic banks is the availability of very limited investment opportunities. In Malaysia for example, initiatives are being taken by the government to introduce an Islamic financial market. This has yet to occur in other Muslim countries.

References and Further Reading

Ahmad, Ziauddin (1994), 'Islamic Banking: State of the Art.' *Islamic Economic Studies*, Vol.2, No.1, pp.1-34.

Ahmed, Osman (1990), 'Sudan: The Role of the Faisal Islamic Bank', in *Islamic Financial Market*, Rodney Wilson (ed), London (UK) & New York (USA), Routledge, pp.76-99.

Ali, Muazzam (1988), 'A Framework of Islamic Banking.' in *Directory of Islamic Financial Institutions*, John R. Presley (ed), London (UK), Croom Helm, pp.3-13.

Aryan, Hossein (1990), 'Iran: The Impact of Islamizationon the Financial System' in *Islamic Financial Market*, Rodney Wilson (ed), London (UK) & New York (USA), Routledge, pp.155-170.

Baldwin, David (1990), 'Turkey: Islamic Banking in a Secularist Context' in *Islamic Financial Market*, Rodney Wilson (ed), London (UK) & New York (USA), Routledge, pp.33-58.

Bank Islam Malaysia Berhad (1984), *Bank Islam: Penubuhan dan Operasi*, Kuala Lumpur (Malaysia).

Bank Negara Malaysia (1994), *Money and Banking in Malaysia*, Kuala Lumpur (Malaysia), Economic Department.

Connors, Jane (1988), 'Towards a System of Islamic Finance in Malaysia.' in *Islamic Law and Finance*, Chibli Mallat (ed), London (UK), Graham & Trotman, pp.57-68

Divine, Thomas F.(1959*)*, *Interest: An Historical & Analytical in Economics and Modern Ethics*, Milwaukee (USA), The Marquette University Press.

El Ashker, Ahmed (1990), 'Egypt: An Evaluation of the Major Islamic Banks.' in *Islamic Financial Market*, Rodney Wilson (ed), London (UK) & New York (USA), Routledge, pp.59-75.

Gieraths, Christine (1990), 'Pakistan: Main Participants and Financial Products of the Islamization Process.' in *Islamic Financial Market*, Rodney Wilson (ed), London (UK) & New York (USA), Routledge, pp.171-195.

Gustave, Glotz (1926), *Ancient Greece at Work, New York*, Alferd A. Knopf.

Hedayati, S.A.A. (1993), *'Islamic Banking as Experienced in the Islamic Republic of Iran.'* A paper presented at the International Conference on Islamic Banking, Sydney (Australia).

Homer, Sidney (1977), *The History of Interest*, 2nd Edition, New Jersey (USA), Rutgers University Press.

Homoud, Sami Hassan (1985), *Islamic Banking: The Adaptation of Banking Practice to Conform with Islamic Law*, London (UK), Arabian Information Ltd.

Homoud, Sami Hassan (1994), 'Progress of Islamic Banking: The Aspirations and the Realities.' *Islamic Economic Studies*, Vol. 2, No. 1 (December), pp.1-80.

International Association of Islamic Banks (undated), *Information booklet*, Jeddah (Saudi Arabia), General Secreteriat.

Iqbal, Zubair and Abbas Mirakhor (1987), *'Islamic Banking'* IMF Occassional Paper No.49, Washington (USA), International Monetary Funds.

Khan, Abdul Jabbar (1990), 'Non-Interest Banking in Pakistan: A Case Study', in *Developing A System of Financial Instruments*, Mohamed Ariff and M.A. Mannan (eds), Jeddah (Saudi Arabia), IRTI, pp.227-243.

Khan, Mohsin S. and **Abbas Mirakhor** (1990), 'Islamic Banking: Experience in the Islamic Republic of Iran and in Pakistan.' *Economic Development & Cultural Change*, Vol.38, No.2 (January), pp.353-375.

Khan, S.R. (1983), *Profit and Loss Sharing: An Economic Analysis of an Islamic Financial System*, Unpublished PhD Dissertation, University of Michigan (USA).

Mirakhor, Abbas (1990), 'The Progress of Islamic Banking: The Case of Iran and Pakistan.' in *Islamic Law and Finance*, Chibli Mallat (ed), London (UK), Graham & Trotman, pp.91-115

Pourian, Heydar. (1993), '*The Problems of a Nationalised, Islamic Financial System: The Case of the Islamic Republic of Iran.*' A paper presented at the International Conference on Islamic Banking, Sydney (Australia).

Ra'ana, Irfan Mahmud (1991), *Economic System Under Umar the Great*, Lahore (Pakistan), SH. Muhammad Ashraf Publisher.

Saeed, Abdullah (1995), 'Islamic Banking in Practive: The Case of Faisal Islamic Bank of Egypt.' *Journal of Arabic, Islamic and Middle Eastern Studies*, Vol.2, No.1, pp.28-46.

Siddiqi, S.A. (1948), *Public Finance in Islam*, reprint 1987, Lahore (Pakistan), SH. Muhammad Ashraf Publisher.

Siddique, Muhammad (1985), *Islamic Banking System: Principles and Practices*, Islamabad (Pakistan), Research Associates.

The Council of Islamic Ideology (Pakistan) (1983), 'Elimination of Interest From the Economy.' in *Money and Banking in Islam*, Ziauddin Ahmed et. al.(eds), Islamabad (Pakistan), Institute of Policy Studies.

The Encyclopaedia of Islam (1971), Vol.1, Lewis, Benard, V.L. Menage, Ch. Pellat, and Joseph Schact (eds), Leiden (Netherlands), E.J. Brill.

The Encyclopedia Americana (1983), Vol.8, Conneticut (USA), Grolier Incorporated.

Wilson, Rodney (1983), *Banking and Finance in the Arab Middle East*, New York (USA), MacMillan Publishers Ltd.

Chapter 2
Theoretical and Conceptual Aspects of Islamic Banking

2.1 Introduction

With more then 10 years of experience, Islamic banks are now in a position of providing almost all basic banking facilities to their customers. Deposit facilities such as current, saving and fixed terms as well as various forms of financing facilities are available in almost all Islamic banks. These banks also serve as pipelines through which currency moves in and out of circulation and, in addition, provide facilities for making domestic and international payments. Some Islamic banks provide more sophisticated facilities such as syndicated loan and also underwrite the issuing of Islamic securities.

Islamic banks are considered as the end product of the Islamic resurgence which started within Islamic communities especially during the end of 1960s and early 1970s. One of the most important issues which was widely discussed during this period was the transformation of the economy from a capitalist to an Islamic economic order. Since the elimination of interest has generally been the first step in the Islamisation of the economy, it is perhaps only natural that the formation and the operation of Islamic banks be given more attention. As an institution whose foundations are based on religious doctrines, the establishment and operations of Islamic banks have raised many theoretical and conceptual considerations. As mentioned by Ali (1988, p.3), *"The 'Islamic Economic Order' is based upon a set of principle found in the Qur'an. No matter what aspect of the Islamic Economic Order is introduced, for practical operations it has to base itself on the Qur'anic concept of social justice. The Islamic financial system, therefore, cannot be introduced merely by eliminating riba but only by adopting the Islamic principles of social justice and introducing laws, practices, procedures and instruments which help in the maintenance and dispensation of justice, equity and fairness."*

Islamic banks therefore are not expected to have similar objectives and philosophies with other business entities. Their objectives and philosophies should be in line with the revelations in the Qur'an and *Hadith* (traditions).

29

The main objective of this chapter is to highlight the philosophies of Islamic business. As a business entity established within the ambit of Islamic law, the Islamic bank is expected to be guided by the philosophy of Islamic business. Establishing the right philosophies is important for any Islamic bank for two reasons. Firstly, these philosophies will be used by the management or policy makers of the banks in the process of formulating corporate objectives and policies. Secondly, these philosophies serve as an indicator as to whether the particular Islamic bank is upholding true Islamic principles. Besides highlighting the general objective of Islamic banks, this chapter will also discuss the relationship between the suppliers and the users of funds, within an Islamic financial system.

2.2 The Philosophy of Islamic Business
Islam permits and encourages its followers to involve in trade activities. As stated in the Qur'an in Verse 275 of Chapter 2:

> *'But Allah hath permitted trade and forbidden usury...'*

The Prophet (*pbuh*) in his early life used to be a trader and, similar to many of his eminent companions, was a businessman. From the religious prospective, the establishment of Islamic banks is considered a righteous move for two reasons. Firstly, its existence is in line with the divine revelation, i.e. to involve in trade. Secondly, Islamic banks provide an avenue for Muslims to perform banking business in the Islamic way, i.e. free from the element of usury.

Eliminating the element of usury in the banking system is only part of Islamic business principles. Being established as an Islamic business entity, all Islamic banks not only have to conduct their business with the objective of making profit but at the same time must conform to Islamic business principles. Islamic banks are also expected to adhere to the rules and laws which are directly imposed on individual Muslims. Otherwise, these entities would not qualify to be called as Islamic entities. This leads one to the philosophical questions: (i) *what should Islamic banks do?* and (ii) *what should they believe?* For Muslims, the answers to these question were given by the Qur'an in many of its verses, Verse 132 of Chapter 3, for example, says:

"Obey Allah and the Messenger; that ye may obtain mercy"

and in Verse 59 of Chapter 4, the Qur'an highlights:

"O ye who believe! Obey Allah, and obey the Messenger...."

Therefore, the foundations of the philosophy of Islamic banking are those principles which have been revealed in the Qur'an and the *Hadith*. Revelations and the *Hadiths* which require Muslims to uphold justice and virtue, serve as principles which guide Islamic banks in managing their business affairs.

The principles of Islamic business comprise of honesty, and trade is to be conducted in a faithful and trustworthy manner. Islam conceives trade as an honest effort, an earnest endeavour, and a human striving for earning one's rightful livelihood. Trade manipulations and malpractices aimed at earning unfair profit through operations like hoarding, black-marketing, profiteering, short-weighting, hiding the defective quality of merchandise, and adulteration cannot be regarded as honest trade (Siddiqi, 1986). The Prophet (*pbuh*) was once conferred a title of '*amin*' or 'the trusted one' because of his honesty in all dealings. The operations of Islamic banks, therefore, are based on the concepts of honesty, justice and equity as practised by the Prophet (*pbuh*).

The meaning of righteous trade can best be understood from the metaphorical content of Chapter 35, Verse 29 of the Qur'an which says:

"Those who rehearse the Book of Allah, establish regular prayer, and send (in charity) out of what We have provided for them, secretly and openly, hope for commerce that will never fail."

The above Verse 29 of Chapter 35 teaches Muslims that the godly man's business will never fail or fluctuate because Allah guarantees him the return, and even adds something to the return out of his own bounty. Analogically, honest trade will lead to the earning of profit in this world as well as in the hereafter. Tarmidzi (d.893AD), reported the Prophet (*pbuh*) as saying, "*The truthful, honest merchant is with the Prophet, truthful and martyrs.*" (Siddiqi, 1986 p.4).

In the process of conducting business, Islamic banks seek to bring about a lasting balance between earning and spending in order to achieve a betterment of the whole community. Islam has always emphasised lawful earning of livelihood. All unlawful means of acquiring wealth are prohibited. Chapter 4, Verses 29 and 30 of the Qur'an states:

"O ye who believe! eat not up your property among yourself in vanities; but let there be amongst you traffic and trade by mutual goodwill; Nor kill (or destroy) yourself: for verily Allah hath been to you most merciful. If any do that in rancour and injustice- soon shall we cast them into fire: and easy it is for Allah."

In terms of spending, Islam demands its followers to spend money for the welfare of the people and not on wasteful or pleasurable activities. This directive is given in Verse 219 of Chapter 2 of the Qur'an which *says*,

"They ask thee concerning wine and gambling. Say, "In them is great sin, and some profit, for men; but the sin is greater than profit". They ask thee how much they are to spend; say "What is beyond your needs". Thus doth Allah makes clear to you his sign; in order ye may consider."

Verse 36 of Chapter 4 of the Qur'an also outlines the right conduct for Muslim and which is applicable for Islamic banks in conducting their business. It says:

"Serve Allah, and join not any partners with Him; and do good to parents, kinsfolk, orphans, those in need, neighbours who are near, neighbours who are strangers, the companion by your side, the wayfarer (ye meet) and what your right hands possess; for Allah loveth not the arrogant, the vainglorious."

In dealing with their customers, Islamic banks are expected to conduct the transactions for the benefit of both, i.e. the banks as well as the customers and uphold the concept of justice. In addition to what was revealed in Chapter 4 Verse 29, Verse 135 of the same chapter says:

"O ye who believe! stand out firmly for justice, as witnesses to Allah, even as against yourself, or your parents, or your kin, and whether it be (against) rich or poor: for Allah can best protect both. Follow not the lusts (of your hearts), lest ye swerve, and if ye distort or decline to do justice, verily Allah is well-acquainted with all that ye do."

Again in Chapter 16 Verse 90, it is stated:

"Allah commands justice, the doing of good, and liberality to kith and kin, and He forbids all shameful deeds, and injustice and rebellion: He instructs you, that ye may receive admonition."

The above mentioned verses require Muslims to uphold justice irrespective of any blood relationship or status. The application of these verses to business context means that Islamic banks must treat their customers equally. This concept of justice is extended by Islamic banks when imposing charges to customers and also when fixing the profit-sharing ratio either with their investors or with their business partners. This philosophy is also reinforced by Verse 87 of Chapter 5, of the Qur'an:

"O ye who believe! make not unlawful the good things which Allah hath made lawful for you, but commit no excess; for Allah loveth not those given to excess."

Mannan (1986) is of the opinion that, in an Islamic social system, welfare is maximised only if economic resources are so allocated that it is impossible to make any one individual better off by any rearrangement without making anyone or some others worse off within the framework of the Qur'an and *Hadith*. Anything which is not expressly prohibited in the *Qur'an* and *Hadith* but is consistent with the spirit of the same may be styled as Islamic. Mannan (1986) therefore, argued that it is not harmful for Islamic banks to undertake such activities.

In Islam, the absolute ownership of everything belongs to Allah. As stated in Verse 189 of Chapter 3:

"To Allah belongeth the dominion of the heavens and the earth; And Allah hath power over all things."

This absolute ownership does not reflect that Allah has created everything for Himself. On the contrary, it is stated in Verse 29 of Chapter 2 that,

"It is He who hath created for you all things that are on earth; then He turned to the heaven and made them into seven firmaments. And of all things He hath perfect knowledge."

Mannan (1986) claimed that the verse emphasises that what Allah has created belongs collectively to the whole of human society. Legal ownership by the individual, that is to say the right of possession, enjoyment and transfer of property, is recognised and safe guarded in Islam, but all ownership is subject to moral obligation and even animals have the right to share. This moral obligation is stated in Verse 19 of chapter 51 of the Qur'an:

> "And in their wealth and possessions (was remembered) the right of the (needy), Him who asked, and him who (for some reasons) was prevented."

As for Islamic banks, while making profit from business is acceptable, the accumulation of profit without utilisation for the betterment of the community is forbidden. Because of this revelation, Islamic banks are expected to be more sensitive to the needs of society, promote more social welfare programs and activities, and make more contributions towards the needy and the poor.

Islam prohibits accumulation of wealth or its unrestricted possession by individuals exclusively for their self-interest. It is further reiterated that wealth which is earned by the right means should not be hoarded in selfish interest because it would impede the growth in the economy, thus creating social imbalance. Verse 3 of Chapter 180 of the Qur'an, states that:

> "And let not those who covetously withheld of the gifts which Allah hath given them of His Grace, think that it is good for them; nay it will be the worse for them; soon shall the things which they covetously withheld be tied to their necks like a twisted collar."

Again in Verses 1 to 4 of Chapter 104 it is repeated:

> "Woe to every (kind of) scandalmonger and backbiter, who pileth up wealth and layeth it by, thinking that his wealth would make him last forever! By no means, he will be sure to be thrown into that which breaks to pieces."

Three vices mentioned by the above verses are here condemned in the strongest terms: (i) scandal mongering, talking or suggesting evil of men or women by word or innuendo, or behaviour, or mimicry, or sarcasm, or insult; (ii) detracting from their character behind their back, even if the things commented are true, where the motive is evil; (iii) accumulating wealth, not for use and service to those who need it, but in miserly hoards, as if such hoards can prolong the miser's life or give him immortality. Miserliness is itself a kind of scandal (Ali, 1989). The above revelation serves as a reminder to those who manage Islamic banks to be more cautious in managing its assets. As mentioned earlier the wealth of Islamic banks should be spent on the needy and for the betterment of society. Failing to conform with the instructions from Allah, means there is a great possibility that the wealth accumulated by the banks will be destroyed. The destruction may be in the sense that the bank will not be able to make further profit and may ultimately have to cease operations.

The Qur'an in many of its verses indicates the principles which serve as guidance for the Islamic banks in their practical affairs. To involve themselves in business is highly encouraged by Islam but the business must be conducted on the basis of equity and justice. Islamic banks are prevented from engaging themselves in the business forbidden by Islam (examples of such businesses are mentioned at the end of the Section 2.4.2).

2.3 The Objectives of Islamic Banks

As suggested by Khan (1983), the existence of Islamic banks is to promote, foster and develop the banking services and product based on Islamic principles. Islamic banks are also responsible for promoting the establishment of investment companies or other business enterprises as long as the activities of these companies are not forbidden by Islam. The main principles of Islamic banking comprise of prohibition of interest in all forms of transactions, and undertaking business and trade activities on the basis of fair and legitimate profit. Islamic banks are to give *zakat* (alms tax) and to develop an environment which benefits society.

Like any other business entity, Islamic banks are expected to make a profit from their operations. It is considered unjust for Islamic banks if they are unable to provide sufficient returns to the depositors who entrusted their money to Islamic banks (Mirakhor, 1987). Making a profit from business is allowed in Islam. However at the same time Islamic banks are required to recognise the message stated in Verse 87 of Chapter 5 of the Qur'an that prohibits Muslims from committing any excess. Applying this message to banking operations means that Islamic banks are prohibited from making excessive profit at the expense of their customers.

Therefore, while ordinary business institutions are likely to place profit as their primary objectives, Islamic banks have to incorporate both profit and morality into their objectives. This objective is succinctly described by Dar Al-Maal Al-Islamic Trust, the holding company for 25 financial and business companies operating on the basis of *Shariah* in 15 countries around the world:

1. To put before to all Muslims, contemporary Islamic financial services, helping to execute their financial dealings in strict respect of the ethical individual and social values of Islamic *Shariah*, without contravening the heavenly imposed prohibition of dealing in *riba* (interest or usury).

2. To serve all Muslim communities in mobilising and utilising the financial resources needed for their true economic development and prosperity within the principles of Islamic justice assuring the right and obligations of both the individual and the community.

3. To serve the *'Ummat Al Islam'* (Islamic communities) and other nations by strengthening the fraternal bonds through mutually beneficial financial relationships for economic development and the enhanced environment for peace.

Similarly, Bank Islam Malaysia Berhad's (BIMB) corporate objective is to provide banking facilities and services in accordance with Islamic principles to all Muslims as well as the population of Malaysia. The Islamic principles mentioned here are essentially those belonging to the body of *Shariah* rules on commercial transactions that relate to banking and finance. The bank's efforts to provide these banking facilities and services are undertaken within the framework of its viability and capability to continuously grow and expand (BIMB, 1985).

Although most Islamic banks clearly state that their main objective is to provide interest-free banking services (e.g. Jordan Islamic Bank, Kuwait Finance House, and Faysal Islamic Bank of Bahrain), their memorandum and articles of association nevertheless list objectives which are quite similar to the objectives of conventional banks. The

Memorandum and Articles of Associations of Dubai Islamic Bank, also include the following as their objectives:

OBJECTS OF THE COMPANY

The company, established to conduct all its operations on a basis which excludes 'USURY', will have the following objects:

i. To carry on all banking services and operations for its own account and the account of others.

ii. To carry on the business of investment directly, purchase or finance projects or business owned by others. The Company may have relations or enter into partnership with any organisation who carry on the business similar to its own business or who assist in fulfilment of its objects in Dubai or elsewhere. It may buy these organisations or amalgamate or merge with them by legal agreement.

iii. To accept cash deposits of different kinds for safe custody or for investment.

iv. To buy and sell bullions, foreign currencies, and bills of exchange.

v. To finance for short term period against security of commercial papers.

vi. To open credits and grant all banking facilities with or without personal guarantees.

vii. To issue guarantee for the benefit of third parties with or without collateral.

viii. To collect, against fee, transfer orders, drafts, debt certificates, bills of lading and other documents for the account of clients or third parties (Others).

ix. To receive subscriptions relating to Limited Liability Companies to be set up, buy and sell shares for the account of the Company or for the account of third parties.

x. To carry on the business of banking and Savings Account Deposits.

xi. To keep, in safe, every type of currencies and precious metals, securities, parcels and packets, and rent private safes.

xii. To act as trustee and attorney, accept proxies and nominate attorneys.

xiii. To utilise modern electric and electronic accounting equipment in order to speed up operations, save time and ensure accuracy.

To rent the services of such equipment to others.

In general, the Company may deal in all kinds of banking transactions and services and other operations which are in accordance with law, and rules and regulations observed by banks.

The Islami Bank Bangladesh Limited (IBBL), categorically declares that its aim is to introduce a welfare-oriented banking system and also to establish equity and justice in all economic activities. In view of such an objective, this bank is considered one of the leading Islamic banks in promoting social activities. The Bank has established a body called 'Islami Bank Foundation' which provides financial assistance to the poor and needy people through various programs. It also undertakes health care, relief and rehabilitation, education, humanitarian programs and religious activities. This Foundation has also established a modern hospital in Dhaka and centres for socio-economic development of the country (IBBL, 1994).

Faisal Islamic Bank of Kibris (FIBK) is another Islamic bank which is actively involved in social activities. This Bank has established a special financial pool called '*Zakat* and Social Help Funds'. The sources of this special fund come from *zakat* (wealth or alms tax) paid by the bank or other parties and donations. This fund is managed by the Bank under the scrutiny of *Shariah* Supervisory Board. The fund are channelled to various social welfare and religious activities (FIBK, 1993).

2.4 Relationship with the Suppliers and Users of Funds

The status of the relationship between the Islamic banks and its suppliers and the users of funds is dependent on the principles of *Shariah* used in creating that relationship. The status of the relationship with the suppliers of funds can vary widely. It can be that of trustee and beneficiary, debtor and creditor, investor and entrepreneur, and between partners. Similarly, the relationship with the users of fund can comprise of debtor and creditor, investor and entrepreneur, principal and agent, trader and customers, and between partners.

Theoretically, the relationship between Islamic banks and the suppliers and users of funds is bounded by three general principles which dominate the economic behaviour of Muslims. These principles comprise the following (Khaf, 1980):

(i) Belief in the Day of Judgement and life in the hereafter.

(ii) Islamic concept of riches.

(iii) Islamic concept of success.

All the above principles are expected not only to have a significant impact on the decision-making process of Muslims, but also to have influence on their perceptions towards Islamic banks.

2.4.1 Suppliers' Point of View

The first principle mentioned above has an impact on the suppliers' (depositor's) behaviour and their decision making process. The choice of action is not only based on the immediate returns but also in the hereafter. Therefore, the decision to have a banking relationship with Islamic banks is not because of a profit motive but rather to gain the blessings of Allah. One of the ways to gain blessings is to support any program that will improve the Muslim community. Verse 20 of Chapter 9 of the Qur'an states:

> *"Those who believe, and suffer Exile and strive with might and main, in Allah's cause, With their goods and their persons, have the highest rank In the sight of Allah: They are the people Who will achieve (salvation)."*

The word *jihad* or 'strive in the cause of Allah' as indicated by the above verse refers to a form of self-sacrifice. Ali (1989) believed that the essence of self-sacrifice consists of (i) true and sincere faith, and (ii) earnest and ceaseless activity, involving the sacrifice (if need be) of life, person, or property, in the service of Allah. Since Islamic banks operate on an interest-free basis and their establishment is to improve Muslim communities, their existence therefore is in the service of Allah.

In the case of the second principle, Islam has given a clear guideline that wealth is a bounty from Allah and is a tool that may be used for good or for evil. Poverty is, in some instances, associated with disbelief and riches are considered a gift from Allah (Khaf, 1980). Wealth itself is considered as an important means by which man can pave the way for the attainment of his ultimate objective. All persons are exhorted to work to earn a living and to accumulate wealth. Accumulating wealth is considered among the highest blessing bestowed on man and everyone is encouraged to strive for wealth. Verse 10 of Chapter 62 of the Qur'an states:

"And when the Prayer Is finished, then may ye Disperse through the land, And seek of the Bounty Of Allah: and celebrate The Praises of Allah Often (and without stint): That ye may prosper."

The above verse suggests that Muslims must work and acquire wealth upon completion of prayer. The methods of earning, possessing, and disposing of wealth are defined by the *Shariah*.

The best method in accumulating wealth as defined by *Shariah* is by striving on one's own and not from the income generated by other people's efforts. Striving for your own food is in line with many *Hadith* in which the Prophet (*pbuh*) had given his advice to Muslims followers to work for their own food. For example, the Prophet (*pbuh*) is reported to have said (Sahih Al-Bukhari, Vol 3, pp.162-3):

"Nobody has ever eaten a better meal than that which one has earned by working with one's own hands. The Prophet of Allah, David, used to eat from the earnings of his manual labour."

Therefore, the practice of treating or expecting the returns given by the Islamic bank as one of the main sources of income to support living is inappropriate from the Islamic perspective. The rewards should only be considered as a complimentary income and should have no significant influence on one's financial position.

The Islamic concept of riches also serves as an important factor which influences Muslims' perceptions toward the existence of Islamic banks. The following *Hadiths* give the meaning of richness from the Islamic perspective:

"Abu Hurairah reported Allah's Messenger (pbuh) as saying: Verily Allah does not look to your face and your wealth but He looks to your heart and to your deeds." — (Sahih Muslim, Vol 4, p.1362)

"Abu Hurairah reported that Messenger of Allah (pbuh) said: Richness does not lie in the abundance of (worldly) goods but richness is the richness of the soul (heart, self)." — (Sahih Muslim, Vol 2, p.501)

As indicated by the above *Hadiths*, Islam defines success as the level of obedience to Allah and not as the accumulation of wealth. Service and obedience may be rendered by the positive use of capabilities and resources given by Allah. According to Islamic teachings, if a man really wants to serve Allah, the utilisation of the natural and human resources made available to him is not only a privilege but also a duty and obligation prescribed by Allah. This is in line with Verse 27 of Chapter 8 of the Qur'an which commands Muslims not to betray the trust given by Allah and His Apostle. Applying this principle to a banker-customer relationship would mean that the suppliers of funds should not be discouraged by low profit returns or the overall success of the bank.

In the light of these three principles, Islamic bank customers are expected not to be guided by the profit motive. Instead, the reason for placing their monies with the Islamic banks is more towards getting blessings from Allah and this action is considered the best way in administering the resources given by Allah. Since it is a belief of every Muslim that all properties belong to Allah, returns on their deposits are also considered a gift from Allah irrespective of amount. Similarly, in the case of losses, it is also from Allah.

2.4.2 Users' Point of View

The users of funds should not regard Islamic banks as institutions with a profit motive, nor as a charitable organisation. Instead, they should perceive Islamic banks as a vehicle in promoting and developing the Islamic community. Although Islamic banks are required to assist those who are in need irrespective of whether that person is their customer, this assistance is limited. This is because Islamic banks have responsibilities not only to those in need but also to the suppliers of funds and the entire community. So the assistance provided must be carefully distributed.

Islamic banks are nevertheless expected to be more supportive towards their customers. Customers who face difficulties in meeting loan repayments will not be treated harshly. This is in line with Verse 280 of Chapter 2 of the Qur'an which says:

> "If a debtor is in a difficulty, grant him time till it is easy for him to repay. But if ye remit it by way of charity, that the best for you if ye only knew."

The customers who receive funds from Islamic banks are expected to discharge their liability accordingly. This is in line with Verse 1 of Chapter 5 of the Qur'an which says:

"O ye who believe! Fulfil (all) obligation...."

In relation to entrepreneurs, Islamic banks are expected to be more receptive and pro-active in the process of creating, moulding and developing entrepreneurs. The principle of *mudaraba* (details in Chapter 4) for example, serves as an impetus for creating new entrepreneurs. Those who possess business skills and ideas but who are without capital can turn to Islamic banks for financing. This mode of financing also encourages existing entrepreneurs to undertake projects that involve high risk but are also highly profitable and productive. Entrepreneurs who enjoy *mudaraba* facilities will benefit in two ways. Firstly, they need not worry about repayment. Islamic banks will only get their share from the ex-post profit. In the case of losses, entrepreneurs go unrewarded for their time and effort. The risk of loss is completely borne by the bank. Secondly, as a partner, Islamic banks will extend their full support not only morally and financially but also in the management aspects of the business.

As a result of an on-going relationship with Islamic banks customers tend to become more religious and ethical. Islamic banks are in a good position to mould the users of their funds toward a religious and ethical life. This is effectively done in two ways. Firstly, as an investor the Islamic bank is guided by *Shariah* and funds can only be invested in productive and permissible investments. The Qur'an declares that the following forms of investments are unlawful:

1. Trades that promote obscenity
2. Prostitution and adultery
3. Manufacture, sale and transportation of liquor
4. Making and sale of idols and services rendered in or to pagan places of worship
5. Fortune-telling and drawing lots
6. Business which involves usury.

Secondly, as a trader, Islam has prescribed some principles concerning trade and commerce which must be followed. At any point in time, transactions must be conducted honestly, faithfully and beneficially. The Qur'an also outlines unlawful conducts. Conducts such as bribery, misappropriation, embezzlement of public or private wealth, larceny, unfair use of the property of an orphan, gambling, and short weight and measure are strictly prohibited by Islam.

2.5 Summary

The term 'Islamic banking' means conduct of banking operations in consonance with Islamic teaching. In view of this definition, Islamic banks are not expected to have philosophies and objectives similar to conventional banks. The development of philosophies and objectives are in line with the principles of Islamic business as highlighted in the Qur'an and *Hadith*. Islamic business entities are required to engage themselves in legitimate and lawful business, and to fulfil all obligations and responsibilities. All transactions are based on the concept of honesty, justice and equity. Overspending and wastage are totally prohibited. Wealth must be used in a proper and orderly manner, that is to help the needy, and transactions must be properly executed.

In view of the above business principles, Islamic banks have both profit and moral obligations as their objectives. In Bangladesh, for example, the Islamic bank is actively involved in promoting programs tailored to the needs of the poorest and aims to increase their income and standard of living. This is also the only Islamic bank which has built a hospital which provides services for the lower income group. As for the other Islamic banks, their social activities vary widely. The Jordan Islamic bank, for example, is required to set aside a certain percentage of its net income for the purpose of scientific research and education. This fund is channelled to various higher institutions in Jordan.

The economic behaviours of Muslims are bound by principles which cause the relationship between Islamic banks and their customers to be based on religious foundations rather then purely monetary rewards.

References and Further Reading

Ali, Muazzam (1988), 'A Framework of Islamic Banking.' in *Directory of Islamic Financial Institutions*, John R. Presley (ed), London (UK), Croom Helm, pp.3-13.

Ahmad, Ziauddin (1994), 'Islamic Banking: State of the Art.' *Islamic Economic Studies*, Vol.2, No.1, pp.1-34.

Ali, Abdullah Yusuf (1989), *The Holy Qur'an: Text, Translation and Commentary.*' (New Revised Edition), Maryland (USA), Amana Corporation.

Siddiqi, Muhammad Iqbal (1986), *Model of an Islamic Bank*, Lahore (Pakistan), Kazi Publications.

Mannan, Muhammad Abdul (1986), *Islamic Economics: Theory and Practice (Foundations of Islamic Economics)*, London (UK), Hodder and Stoughton.

Khan, M. Fahim (1983), 'Islamic Banking as Practised Now in the World.' in *Money and Banking in Islam*, Ziauddin Ahmed et. al (eds), Islamabad (Pakistan), Institute of Policy Studies, pp.259-276.

Mirakhor, Abbas (1987), 'Short-term Asset Concentration and Islamic Banking.' in *Theoretical Studies in Islamic Banking and Finance*, Mohsin S. Khan and Abbas Mirakhor (eds), Huston (USA), The Institute for Research in Islamic Studies, pp.185-199.

Faysal Islamic Bank of Bahrain (1993), *Annual Report*, Manama (Bahrain).

Bank Islam Malaysia Berhad (1985), *Annual Report*, Kuala Lumpur (Malaysia).

Dubai Islamic Bank (undated), *Information Leaflet*, Dubai (The United Arab Emirates).

Dubai Islamic Bank (1975), *Memorandum and Articles of Association*, Dubai (The United Arab Emirates).

Government of Jordan (1978), *Jordan Islamic Bank for Finance and Investment Law No.13 of 1978*, Amman (Jordan).

Kuwait Finance House (1977), *Memorandum of Agreement and Articles of Association*, Safa (Kuwait).

Islami Bank Bangladesh Limited (1994), *Annual Report*, Dhaka (Bangladesh).

Faisal Islamic Bank of Kibris (1993), *Annual Report*, Mersin (Turkey).

Khaf, Monzer (1986), 'A Contribution to the Theory of Consumer Behaviour in an Islamic Society.' in *Studies in Islamic Economics*, Kurshid Ahmad (ed), Islamic Foundation, Leicester (UK), pp.19-36.

Khan, Muhammad Muhsin (1977), *The Translation of the Meanings of Sahih Al-Bukhari* (6th Edition), Vol. 3, Lahore (Pakistan), Kazi Publications.

Chapter 3
Prohibition of *Riba* in Islam

3.1 Introduction

The most important aspect of Islamic banking is that its operations must be conducted without any element of *riba*.. The question here is, why Islam tends to be so harsh and intolerable with *riba*, whereas, accepting and paying interest is an acceptable and common practice to other communities. Those who are used to the conventional banking system may believe that interest is the 'life blood' of the entire banking system. Without interest, it is argued the system would grind to a halt (Mannan, 1986).

In the past there has been some disputes amongst the Muslim scholars about whether *Riba* refers to interest or usury. Some scholars have argued that what Islam prohibits is usury and not interest. They claimed that interest paid on loans for investment in productive activities would not contravene the Qur'an for it refers only to usury on non-productive loans which prevailed in pre-Islamic times when people were not familiar with productive loans and its influence on economic development. In Islam, there is no segregation between interest and usury. There is now general consensus among Muslim scholars and theologians that the term *Riba* covers both interest and usury (Khan, 1987).

Islam condemns those who associate themselves with the practice of *riba*. The Qur'an explicitly states that the charging of interest will draw a declaration of war from Allah and His Messenger and promises total destruction of an economy which allows interest-based transactions. The objective of this chapter is to illustrate *riba* from the Islamic perspective.

3.2 Meaning of *Riba*

Riba is an Arabic word which literally means 'increase' (*al-ziyada*), 'growth' (*al-numuw*), 'to rise' and 'to become lofty' (*al-irtifa* and *al-uluw*) (Ahmad, 1992). From the *Shariah* (Islamic law) point of view, however, *riba* technically refers to the 'premium' that must be paid by the borrower to the lender along with the principle amount as a condition for the loan or for an extension on its maturity (Chapra, 1992). Taking this definition into consideration, therefore, we conclude that

45

riba and interest are the same thing and can be used interchangeably. As stated earlier, Islam does not segregate between interest and usury. Linguistically, *riba* means 'increase' and 'growth'. Ibn Manzur (1233-1311) in his *Lissanul Arab* states, "*The root of it is the increase, of the riba of money where it has increased.*" Tabari (d.923), an interpreter gave his opinion that the word "*rabia*" or hill was thus called because it is greater in height and overlooks the ground around it. The meaning of *riba* can also be applied to two different contexts. First, it could be an increase to the thing itself and second, it could be an increase resulting from comparison or difference between two things (Homoud, 1985).

The term *riba* was also used by pre-Islamic Arabs. According to them *riba* was what they dealt in on the basis of increase of money in consideration of extension in terms of maturity. Therefore, contemporary Muslim scholars tend to link the word *riba* with loan and retain this pre-Islamic meaning of *riba*. Khan (1987, p.3) defines *riba* as, "*.... the addition to the amount of principal of loan on the basis of time for which it is loaned, or of the time for which the payment is deferred.*"

According to Saleh (1986, p.13), "*Riba in its Shariah context, can be defined, as generally agreed, as an unlawful gain derived from the quantitative inequality of the countervalues in any transaction purporting to effect the exchange of two or more species (anwa', singular, naw'), which belong to the same genus (jins) and are governed by the same efficient cause ('illa, plural, 'ilal). Deferred completion of the exchange of such species, or even of species which belong to different genera but are governed by the same 'illa, is also riba, whether or not the deferment is accompanied by an increase in any one of the exchanged countervalues.*"

3.3 The Prohibition of *Riba*

Muslims are totally prohibited from dealing with *riba*. Ahmad (1992) claimed that there should not be two opinions on the categorical prohibition of *riba* in Islam. The difference according to him lies in the interpretation of its scope and coverage. The prohibition of *riba* is not only revealed in various Verses of the Qur'an but is also reinforced by the Prophet (*pbuh*) who uses unambiguous words in condemning the accepter and the provider of *riba*.

3.3.1 The Prohibition of *Riba* in the Qur'an

The prohibition of *riba* in the Qur'an developed gradually. It first appeared in Verse 39 of Chapter *al-Rum* which was revealed during the Meccan period.

First revelation: *al-Rum*, Verse 39 (30:39),

> *"That which ye lay out For increase through the property of (other) people, will have No increase with Allah: But that which ye lay out For charity, seeking The Countenance of Allah, (Will increase): it is These who will get A recompense multiplied."*

The word 'increase' in the above Verse is interchangeable with the word *riba* and therefore, Muslims are strongly recommended not to deal in *riba*. The purport is that any profit sought by Muslims should be through their own exertion and not through exploitation of others or at the expense of others. Muslims must also show their love for their neighbours by spending their own resources or by the utilisation of their own talents and opportunities in the service of those who need them. When this Verse was revealed, the city of Mecca was prosperous with business and trade. The Meccans were not only actively involved in import, export and facilitated the transit of goods, but participated in loans for interest, speculations and aleatory transactions. These activities were performed because of their unwillingness to see their capital being unproductive while awaiting the departure or arrival of caravans (Saleh, 1986). The other three revelations that were revealed in Medina are in the Chapter *al-Nisa'* Verse 161, Chapter *Al' Imran* Verses 130 to 132, and Chapter *al-Baqarah* Verses 275 to 281. These three revelations are even clearer about the condemnation of *riba*.

Second revelation: *al-Nisa'*, Verse 161 (4:161),

> *"That they took usury, Though they were forbidden; And that they devoured Men's substance wrongfully - We have prepared for those Among them who reject Faith A grievous punishment."*

The second revelation created some misunderstanding among the Muslim jurists as to whether the prohibition was directed to Muslims or to the Jews. These misunderstandings occurred because immediately before this Verse, Verse 160 states,

"For the iniquity of the Jews We made unlawful for them Certain (foods) good and wholesome Which had been lawful for them - In that they hindered many From Allah's way -."

Hitti (1970), a contemporary historian believed that Verse 161 of *Al-Nisa* was directed to Medinan Jews. Saleh (1986) opposed Hitti's view and argued that the discontentment with *riba* first occurred while the Prophet (*pbuh*) was still in Mecca and Jews were very few at that time. Another reason given by Saleh was that the Jews in Medina in those times were mostly involved in the agricultural sector and not in the commercial sector. It was the *Muhajirun* (Meccans who accompanied the Prophet (*pbuh*) in his migration to Medina) and *Ansar* (the Medinan Muslims) who dealt with usury in Medina. To support his argument Saleh used two statements given by Abu Huraira (d.678AD) and Abdullah Ibn Salam (d.663/4AD). Both of them were '*sahaba*' or 'companions' of the Prophet (*pbuh*). Abu Huraira said, *"You people say that Abu Huraira tells many narrations from Allah's Apostle (pbuh) and you also wonder why the emigrants and Ansar do not narrate from Allah's Apostle (pbuh) as Abu Huraira does. My emigrant brothers were busy in the market while I used to stick to Allah's Apostle (pbuh) content with that which fills my stomach: So I used to be present when they were absent and I used to remember when they used to forget, and my Ansari brothers used to be busy with their properties and I was one of the poor men of Suffa. I used to remember the narrations when they used to forget. ....."* (Sahih Bukhari, Vol.3, p.149). Abdullah Ibn Salam said that *riba* was widespread throughout Medina, and that was interpreted as being the case even after the Prophet's death and after the ejection of Jews.

Third revelation: *Al' Imran*, Verses 130-2 (3:130-2)

"O ye who believe! Devour not Usury, Double and multiplied; But fear Allah; that Ye may (really) prosper."
"Fear the Fire, which is prepared For those who reject Faith;"
"And obey Allah And The Messenger; That ye may obtain mercy."

The above prohibition was revealed in the wake of the battle of Uhud that took place in the third year of *Hijrah*. Some scholars argue of a relationship between this Verse and the preceding Verse, where the polytheists had spent money on soldiers who fought in the said battle.

This money was raised by practising *riba*. Another possibility was that the Muslims might be tempted to practise *riba* in order to raise money and spend it on soldiers who revenged from the polytheists.

The verse also indicates that the prohibition is for all forms and kinds of *riba*. The words double and multiple, however, did create anomalies among Muslim jurists and scholars. Scholars believe that the ban in this verse is no more than a partial one relative to excessive *riba* that keeps increasing until it becomes multiple or multiples. According to Quttub (1906-1966) the terms used were no more than a state of affairs and not a condition relevant to the imposition. Abdo (1849-1905) a jurist from Egypt claimed that it is not a condition of usury that the capital sum must multiply as to render the one hundred to two hundred, but usury (which is the increase) multiplies by repetition.

Shaltut (1974) in his response to those who believed that the ban in this verse is for the excessive riba states, "This statement is null and void as when Allah said "multiple of multiples" He meant to reprimand them for what they were doing and to emphasise and condemn their evil doings. A similar style was adopted where Allah said, "do not force your girls to commit prostitution if they to be immune against it, in an urge to obtain the property—other than dinars and dirhams—of life in this world." The aim here is not to ban them (the Muslims) from forcing girls to commit prostitution if they wish to be immunised against it nor to allow them to commit prostitution if the girls do not wish immunisation against it, but the intention is to vilify and condemn their doings. The same thing applies to the verse of usury." (Quoted from Homoud, 1985 p.71).

The current consensus is that the ban intended in this verse covers all forms of *riba* regardless of whether the numbers, amounts or percentages involved are double or multiple. This absolute prohibition is later confirmed by Verses in the Chapter of *al-Baqarah* in which Allah describes the creditor's right to recover no more than his capital is highlighted.

Fourth revelation: *al-Baqarah*, Verses 275-81 (2:275-81),

> *"Those who devour usury Will not stand except As stands one whom The Evil One by his touch Hath driven to madness. That is because they say: "Trade is like usury," But Allah hath permitted trade And forbidden usury. Those who after receiving Direction from their Lord,*

Desist, shall be pardoned For the past; their case Is for Allah (to judge); But those who repeat (The offence) are Companions of the Fire; they will Abide therein (forever)."

"Allah will deprive Usury of all blessing, But will give increase For deeds of charity; For He loveth not Creatures ungrateful And wicked."

"Those who believe, And do deeds of righteousness, And establish regular prayers And regular charity, Will have their reward With their Lord: On them shall be no fear, Nor shall they grieve."

"O ye who believe! Fear Allah, and give up What remains of your demand For usury, if ye are Indeed believers."

"If ye do it not, Take notice of war from Allah and His Messenger: But if ye turn back, Ye shall have Your capital sums; Deal not unjustly, And ye shall not Be dealt with unjustly."

"If the debtor is In a difficulty, Grant him time Till it is easy For him to repay. But if ye remit it By way of charity, That is best for you If ye only knew."

"And fear the Day When ye shall be Brought back to Allah. Then shall every soul Be paid what it earned, And none shall be Dealt with unjustly."

The above Verses of *al-Baqarah* which were revealed in Thaqeef near the completion of the Prophet's *(pbuh)* mission severely condemned those who deal in *riba*. Verse 275 specifically mentions that there is a difference between trade and usury *(riba)*. While trade is permissible, usury is forbidden. The word 'stand' which is written as 'rise' by some translators in the first Verse has two meanings. Some scholars believe that the word is a description of the state of those who take *riba* on the day of judgement, whereas others believe that the word has nothing to do with the day of judgement. This word they said is for those (usurers) who 'cling greedily' to the worldly trade and this attitude causes disruption in their life. According to Homoud (1985), it is possible to combine both trends, because such combination does not create a conflict, in that where a person disobeys Allah's orders, he becomes miserable in this world and the life hereafter. This position is also in conjunction with Verse 72 of the Chapter *Al-Isra'*, which says;

"But those who were blind In this world, will be Blind in the Hereafter, And most astray From the Path."

In the Verses 276 and 277, it is reminded that those who take *riba* will not be blessed by Allah, or Allah will destroy property which has the element of *riba* in it. In this case the destruction of property may be in this real world or in the next world. Similarly, as explained in the above paragraph, the individual who deals in *riba* will be punished in both worlds. In the subsequent verse, it is reminded that Muslims must fear Allah and abandon the remnence of the *riba* that occurred during the pre-Islamic days. Inability to comply with this instruction will bring war from Allah and His messenger. This statement serves as a serious warning to Muslims that they should not associate themselves with *riba*. They are allowed to demand from borrowers the principal sum only with no more and no less. Muslims are also urged to deal justly and fairly with the debtors. In case of debtors being unable to repay their debt, the lender is given two alternatives. First they should extend the repayment date or duration of loan. Alternatively they should convert the loan to charity. Among the two options, it is suggested that the second option is the better for Muslims.

3.3.2 The Prohibition of *Riba* in The *Hadith*

As the original and eternal source of *Shariah* law, the Qur'an neither defines *riba* nor does it mention the dealing that comes under it (Ahmad, 1992). The prohibitions of *riba* revealed in four Chapters of Qur'an serve as universal and fundamental guidelines for Muslims. The *Hadith* on the other hand, serves as a source of reference for Muslims to confirm or to get further elaboration on the rules stipulated in the Qur'an. The *Hadiths* are reported in numerous accounts and sometimes differ according to the narrator.

The *Hadith* which relates to *riba* can be classified into three, namely 'directive *Hadith*,' 'explanatory *Hadith*,' and 'reminder *Hadith*.' A directive *Hadith* is that which prevents Muslims from dealing in any kind of *riba*. Explanatory *Hadith* is that which explains the types and the circumstances of trade that would generate *riba*. Reminder *Hadith* visualises the consequences of those who associate themselves with the practice of *riba*. This classification, however, is not absolute. Some *Hadiths* are dual in nature. For example, the famous *Hadith* where the Prophet (*pbuh*) said, "Gold for gold, silver for silver.....," can either be a directive or an explanatory *Hadith*. Below are examples of *Hadiths* in the three mentioned categories.

Directive Hadith

1. "If they accept, well and good and, failing which warn them of war." - This *Hadith* is from the Prophet's letter to his governor of Mecca, Itab ben Osaid when Thaqeef claimed their debts from Bani Mogheera. — (Homoud, 1985, p.80)

2. "O People, just as you regard this month, this day, this city as Sacred, so regard the life and property of every Muslim as a sacred trust. Return the goods as entrusted to you to their rightful owner. Hurt no one so that no one may hurt you. Remember that you will indeed meet your Lord, and that He will indeed reckon your deeds. Allah has forbidden you to take *riba*, therefore all *riba* obligation shall henceforth be waived. Your capital, however, is yours to keep. You will neither inflict nor suffer inequity. Allah has judged that there shall be no *riba* and that all the *riba* due to Abbas ibn' Abd'al Muttalib shall henceforth be waived." This *Hadith* is from the last sermon which was delivered by the Prophet (*pbuh*) on the Ninth day of Dzul Hijjah 10 AH (after *hijrah*). — (Chapra, 1992, p.380)

3. Narrated by 'Aun bin Abu Juhaifa: My father bought a slave who practised the profession of cupping. (My father broke the slave's instruments of cupping). I asked my father why he had done so. He replied, "The Prophet (*pbuh*) forbade the acceptance of the price of a dog or blood, and also forbade the profession of tattooing, getting tattooed and receiving or giving *riba*, and cursed the picture-makers" — (Khan, 1986, p.169)

Explanatory Hadith

1. Narrated by Ibn Shihab that Malik bin Aus said, "I was in need of change for one-hundred Dinars. Talha bin 'Ubaid-Ullah called me and we discussed the matter, and he agreed to change (my Dinars). He took the gold pieces in his hand and fidgeted with them, and then said, "Wait till my storekeeper comes from the forest." Umar was listening to that and said, "By Allah! You should not separate from Talha till you get the money

from him, for Allah's Apostle (*pbuh*) said, "The selling of gold for gold is *riba* except if the exchange is from hand to hand and equal in amount, and similarly, the selling of wheat for wheat is *riba* unless it is from hand to hand and equal amount, and the selling of barley for barley is *riba* unless it is from hand to hand and equal in amount, and dates for dates, is *riba* unless it is from hand to hand and equal in amount." — (Khan, 1986, p.211)

2. "Don't sell gold for gold unless equal in weight, nor silver for silver unless equal in weight, but you could sell gold for silver or silver for gold as you like." Narrated by Abu Bakra. — (Khan, 1986, p.210)

3. Narrated by Abu Said Al-Khudri and Abu Huraira: Allah's Apostle (*pbuh*) appointed somebody as a governor of Khaibar. That governor brought to him an excellent kind of dates (from khaibar). The Prophet (*pbuh*) asked, "Are all the dates of Khaibar like this?" He replied, "By Allah, no, O Allah's Apostle! But we barter one *Sa* of this (type of dates) for two *Sa*'s of dates of ours and two *Sa*'s of it for three of ours." Allah's Apostle (*pbuh*) said, "Do not do so (as that is a kind of usury) but sell the mixed dates (of inferior quality) for money, and then buy good dates with that money." — (Khan, 1986, p.222)

4. "Do not sell gold for gold unless equivalent in weight, and do not sell less amount for greater amount or vice versa; and do not sell silver for silver unless equivalent in weight, and do not sell less amount for greater amount or vice versa and do not sell gold for silver that is not present at the moment of exchange for gold or silver that is present." Narrated by Abu Said Al-Khudri. — (Khan, 1986, p.213)

5. Narrated by Abu Salih Az-Zaiyat: I heard Abu Said Al-Khudri saying, "The selling of a Dinar for a Dinar, and a Dirham for a Dirham (is permissible)." I said to him, "Ibn Abbas does not say the same." Abu Said replied, "I asked Ibn Abbas whether he had heard it from the Prophet (*pbuh*) or seen it in the Holy Book. Ibn Abbas replied, "I do not claim that, and you know Allah's Apostle (*pbuh*) better than I, but Usama informed me that Prophet (*pbuh*) had said, "There is no *riba* (in money ex-

change) except when it is not done from hand to hand (i.e., when there is delay in payment)." — (Khan, 1986, p.213)

6. Narrated by Abu Said al-Khudri: Once Bilal brought Barni (i.e., a kind of dates) to the Prophet (*pbuh*) and the Prophet (*pbuh*) asked him, "From where have you brought these?" Bilal replied, "I had some inferior dates and exchanged two *Sa*'s of it for one *Sa* of Barni dates in order to give it to the Prophet (*pbuh*) to eat." Thereupon the Prophet (*pbuh*) said, "Beware! Beware! This is definitely *riba* ! This is definitely *riba* ! Don't do so, but if you want to buy (a superior kind of dates) sell the inferior dates for money and then buy the superior kind of dates with that money." — (Khan, 1986, p.291)

6. Narrated by Abu Al-Minhal: I asked Al-Bara bin Azib and Zaid bin Arqam about money exchanges. Each of them said,"This is better than I," and both of them said, "Allah's Apostle (*pbuh*) forbade the selling of silver for gold on credit." — (Khan, 1986, p.213)

7. Narrated by Abdur-Rahman bin Abu Bakra that his father said, "The Prophet (*pbuh*) forbade the selling of gold for gold and silver for silver except if they are equivalent in weight, and allowed us to sell gold for silver and vice versa as we wished." — (Khan, 1986, p.214)

8. "Gold for gold, silver for silver, wheat for wheat, barley for barley, dates for dates, and salt for salt - like for like, equal for equal, and hand for hand; if the commodities differ, then you may sell as you wish, provided that the exchange is hand-to-hand." Narrated by Ubada ibn al-Samit. — (Chapra, 1992, p.383)

Reminder Hadith

1. "This night I dreamt that two men came and took me to a holy land whence we proceeded on till we reached a river of blood, where a man was standing, and on its bank was standing another man with stones in his hands. The man in the middle of the river tried to come out, but the other threw a stone in his mouth and forced him to go back to his original place. So, whenever he tried to come out, the other men would throw a

stone in his mouth and force him to go back to his former place. I asked, "Who is this?" I was told, "The person in the river was a *riba*-eater." Narrated by Samura bin Jundab. — (Khan, 1986, pp.168-169)

2. "On the night of Ascension I came upon people whose stomachs were like houses with snakes visible from the outside. I asked Gabriel who they were. He replied that they were people who had received interest." Narrated by Abu Huraira. — (Chapra, 1992, p.381)

3. "A Dirham of *riba* which a man receives knowingly is worse than committing adultery thirty-six times." Narrated by 'Abdallah ibn Hanzalah. — (Chapra, 1992, p.381)

4. "*Riba* has seventy segments, the least serious being equivalent to a man committing adultery with his own mother." Narrated by Abu Hurairah. — (Chapra, 1992, p.381)

5. "There will certainly come a time for mankind when everyone will take *riba* and if he does not do so, its dust will reach him." Narrated by Abu Hurairah. — (Chapra, 1992, p.381)

6. "Allah would be justified in not allowing four persons to enter heaven or to taste its blessings: he who drinks habitually, he who takes *riba*, he who usurps orphan's property without right, and he who is undutiful to his parents." Narrated by Abu Hurairah. — (Chapra, 1992, p.383)

7. "Whoever makes a recommendation for his brother and accepts a gift offered by him has entered *riba* through one of its large gates." Narrated by Abu Ummah. — (Chapra, 1992, p.384)

3.4. The Classification of *Riba*

Although there are numerous types of *riba*, there is no standardisation among the earlier and contemporary Muslim scholars in classifying them. The method of classification, however, can easily be divided based on the following:

i.   The time of occurrence.
ii. The source of prohibition.
iii. The nature of transaction that can generate *riba*.

The easiest classification of *riba* tends to be based on time and is called 'pre-Islamic *riba*'. This term is widely used by early as well as contemporary Muslim writers in describing the *riba* which had been in existence prior to the introduction of Islam to Arabs. This pre-Islamic *riba* is also known as '*riba al-jahiliyya*' to some writers. *Riba al-jahiliyya* refers to the practice of increasing the amount of debt as a result of extension on the term of maturity, either from the date of maturity or from the actual date of debt. The meaning of this term is in line with the opinion given by early Muslims scholars. Tabari in his interpretation of *riba* mentioned, "In pre-Islamic times where a man was indebted to another he used to say: I give you so much if you extend the date for payment whereupon the creditor extends the date of payment " (Homoud, 1985).

Fakhr al-Din Razi (1149-1209), in his deliberation about the business practices of pre-Islamic Arabs believed that Arabs in debt used to pay money monthly and left the principal amount intact. On maturity the debtor had to pay the principal amount. Therefore, in case of inability to repay, the creditor would increase the principal and extend the term. This additional amount according to Razi had been called *riba* in the pre-Islamic times.

Since the prohibitions of *riba* that occurred during the pre-Islamic period came from the Qur'an, this *riba* is also referred to as '*riba Al-Quran*'. Tabari believed that the prohibition of *riba* in the Qur'an referred to the pre-Islamic *riba*. This type of *riba* covered the practice of deferring debt with the additional condition of an increase in the amount of repayment. According to Tabari, the meaning of Verse 130 of Chapter *Al Imran* refers to the *riba* that people dealt with during the pre-Islamic days (Homoud, 1985). The practice of increasing the amount of debt due to an extension in maturity is also known as *dayn mu'ajjal*. Ahmad (1992) argued that Tabari's statement created an ambiguity in two areas. First, it was unclear whether *dayn mu'ajjal* originated from sale transactions or from loan dealings, and second whether the stipulation of *riba* occurred in the first term or during subsequent terms. Ahmad concluded that the *dayn mu'ajjal* originated principally from the practice of *bay' bi'l-nasiah* i.e. credit sale with a fixed term (trade credit) to the agreed price. This usually resulted in *riba* dealings which caused the multiplication of the debt (deferred price).

Ismail (1992) referred to the works of Ibn al-Arabi (d.n.a.), Al-Qurtubi (d.n.a.) and Al-Jassas (d.n.a.) in his discussion on deferred contracts of exchange, mentioned in the Qur'an. He concluded that the word *riba* which was unanimously agreed to by the three exegetists was known as *'riba al-Duyun'*. The *'riba al-Duyun'* can also be divided into two i.e., *'riba al-Jahiliyyah'* and *'riba al-Qardah'*. The *'riba al-Jahiliyyah'* according to Ismail arises when the creditor in a deferred contract of exchange either in a *al-Bai Bithaman ajil* (deferred sale), *bai' al-Istisna* (sale on order), or *al-Ijarah* (leasing) demands from the debtor an additional amount over and above that which was initially agreed to in the original contract. The *'riba al-Qardah'* is a similar additional consideration of time, applicable only in the case of loans and not for contract of exchange.

Another classification of *riba* is called 'post-Islamic *riba*' or widely known as 'sales *riba*'. Jassas (d.n.a.) described that a form of *riba* which was unknown to the pre-Islamic Arabs is the 'sales *riba*'. The prohibition of this type of *riba* came from the *Hadith* of Prophet (*pbuh*) which involved the exchanges of six specific items which are gold, silver, wheat, barley, dates and salt. This *riba* is also known as *'riba al-sunnah'*.

Sales *riba* can be further divided into two, 'increased *riba*' and 'delayed payment *riba*'. *Riba* is committed where the following elements are satisfied (Homoud, 1985 pp.85-86):

Increased *riba*:
i.   There must be a sale where items of the same kind are exchanged;
ii. Both goods must be items subject to *riba* which are mentioned in the *Hadiths*, or accessories, although there is indifference in opinion in this regard; and
iii. There must be an increase in weight or measure in either one of the goods inspite of a difference in the quality of the items exchanged.

Delayed payment *riba*:
i.   There must be a sale;
ii. That both goods are property items subject to *riba* where the cause is common to both of them;
iii. That either consideration is received but/not the other.

The Arabic terms that are frequently used by modern scholars in elaborating *riba* in Islam are '*riba al-nasiah*' and '*riba al-fadl*'. The word *nasiah* comes from the root *nasa'a* which means 'to postpone', 'defer' or 'wait', and it refers to the time that is allowed for the borrower to repay the loan after its due date. In return, the borrower must pay the additional amount or premium for the extension in duration and that additional amount is considered to be *riba*. Therefore, *riba al-nasiah* is the *riba* which has occurred since pre-Islamic days and which is forbidden by the Qur'an. In other words, *riba al-nasiah* is the *riba al-jahiliyyah* with different writers using different terminology. This *riba* is also the *riba* which was mentioned by the Prophet (*pbuh*) in the *Hadith* narrated by Usama Ibn Zayd, "*There is no riba except in nasiah.*" (Chapra, 1992 p.35). The *riba al-nasiah* is also known as '*riba al-duyun*' or '*riba al-mubashir*', or '*riba al-jali*'.

Riba al-fadl is the *riba* which occurs as a result of trade or sale transactions. It covers all spot transactions involving cash payment and immediate delivery of the commodity. The prohibition of this kind of *riba* is covered by the *Hadith* that states, "*gold for gold, and silver for silver........*" This *riba* is what Muslim scholars have termed as 'sales *riba*' or '*riba al-sunnah*'. This *riba* is also known as '*riba al-buyu*', or '*riba ghyr al-mubashir*', or '*riba al-Khafi*'. (Chapra, 1992).

Generally, one can conclude that the 'pre-Islamic *riba*' originated from debt. This debt, can in turn originate from two sources, namely, business (credit transactions) and straight loans. The 'post-Islamic *riba*' originated from sales and this *riba* must have been the result of either unbalance in value or quantity of the goods involved in the exchange process or the increase in price as a result of deferment of payment. It must be noted that the debt *riba* that occurred during the pre-Islamic period did not necessarily cease to exist during the post-Islamic period. In other words the *riba* of direct loans although considered a pre-Islamic *riba* continued to occur even during the post-Islamic period. A summary of the classification of *riba* is shown in Table 3.1 below.

Table 3.1
Classification of *Riba*

	Pre-Islamic *Riba*	Post-Islamic *Riba*
Source of Prohibition	Qur'an	*Hadith*
Area of Emergence	Extension of Debt	Point of Sales: Increase in countervalues Delay in payment
Common Terminology	Debt *riba* *Riba Al-Quran* *Riba al-jahiliyya* *Riba al-nasiah* *Riba al-duyun* *Riba al-mubashir* *Riba al-jali*	Sales *riba* *Riba al-Hadith* *Riba al-sunnah* *Riba al-fadl* *Riba al-buyu* *Riba ghyr al-mubashir* *Riba al-khafi*

3.5   *Riba* Among The Muslims

Unlike amongst Christians who had been engaged in a long debate that ended with the issuance of a decree that legalised the taking of interest, Muslims do not seem to be involved in such controversy. There are a few possible reasons that have prevented Muslims from involving in such a debate. First, the Qur'an has given a clear guideline concerning the prohibition of interest. Secondly, Muslims in the early days, had the opportunity to obtain clarification or guidance on this matter from the Prophet (*pbuh*). The Prophet (*pbuh*) himself on several occasions made specific remarks on this matter. The *khalifa* (caliphs—the successors of the prophet) also commented on *riba*. For example, Umar (the second caliph) on listening to the discussion between Malik bin Aus and Talha bin Ubaidullah intervened by mentioning their wrongdoing and quoted the Prophet's words (refer to explanatory *Hadith* in section 3.3.2). Similarly, Umar also set an example by not taking the delicious dates as a gift from the borrower and mentioned that receiving a gift from the borrower was in fact considered *riba* even when the gift is unrelated to the loan but is given at the commencement of the loan period.

In view of such instances, there is little controversy with regards to the doctrine of *riba*. On one occasion, however, there was indeed some confusion among the early Muslims. It was reported that Ibn Abbas (d.686-8) and Abu Said Khudri (d.694/6) had some misunderstanding about sales *riba*. Abu Said warned Ibn Abbas by saying, *"Oh ye Ibn Abbas, until when would you let people eat riba; did you accompany the Prophet (pbuh), as no one else did; did you hear from him what was not heard by anyone else ?"* Ibn Abbas replied, *"No, but Ussama ben Zaid related to me that the Prophet (pbuh) said that there is no riba except in delayed payment."* Then Abu Said said, *"By God, I will not stay with you under the same roof so long as you persist in this say."* (Homoud, 1985, p.82).

Although the discussion on *riba* among Muslims has yet to reach a final conclusion, this does not mean that *riba* is a less significant matter among Muslims. On the contrary, jurists of all four Muslim *mazaheb* (schools of thought) have discussed this matter and have issued specific guidelines to be followed by their members. There are, however, some slight differences among the *mazaheb* with regard to the areas such as the scope of the ban of *riba*, the transactions that constitute *riba*, and types of property which are subjected to *riba*, but not on *riba* itself.

3.5.1 The Views of Various *Mazaheb*

Mazaheb (sing. *mazahab*) or 'schools of religious law' were the bodies which played an important role in developing Islamic jurisprudence. These schools of law had their origin in the late seventh century as scholars committed to legal doctrines and methods of legal analysis differed in opinions. Although many schools were formed during those periods, only four such schools have survived till present. These schools are the Hanafis, Malikis, Shafiis, and Hanbalis.

With regards to the debt *riba*, there is an agreement among them that every loan that produces an advantage is *riba*. *Riba*, however, is not committed in the case of an additional amount paid by the debtor over the principal sum if there is no expressed agreement which requires the debtor to do so. This is in line with the *Hadith* narrated by Abu Huraira where the Prophet (*pbuh*) said, *"The best of you is he who re-pays best."*

There were some differences in opinion among the *mazaheb* in relation to the Prophet's *Hadith* that says, *"Gold for gold, silver for silver, wheat for wheat ...."* Since the scope of this book is limited to Islamic banking, it is not our intention to discuss the opinions of various schools of thought on sales *riba* in great detail. Nevertheless, for the benefit of readers a summary of opinions of all schools of law are given in Table 3.2.

Table 3.2
Summary of Opinions of Various Mazaheb on *Riba*

Nature of Transactions	Opinions
Hanafis:	
a. The exchanged countervalues are all measurable or all weighable and belong to the same genus, as the sale of wheat for wheat.	No gain permitted in a hand-to-hand transaction and no deferred transaction, even without gain.
b. The exchanged countervalues are all measurable or all weighable but belong to different genera, such as sale of gold for silver.	No deferred transaction permitted, even without gain. Increase permissible in a hand-to-hand transaction.
c. The exchanged countervalues are not measurable or weighable but belong to the same genus, such as the sale of an animal for an animal.	No deferred transaction permitted even without gain. Gain permissible in a hand-to-hand transaction.
d. One of the exchanged countervalues is measurable while the other is not (whether weighable or not), such as the sale of wheat for silver or pomegranates, or	Gain permissible whether in a hand-to-hand transaction or in a deferred one.
e. One of the exchanged countervalues is weighable while the other is not (whether measurable or not), such as the sale of gold for wheat or quinces.	Gain permissible whether in a hand-to-hand transaction or in a deferred one.
f. The exchanged countervalues are not measurable or weighable, and furthermore belong to different genera, such as the sale of pomegranates for quinces.	Gain permissible whether in a hand-to-hand transaction or in a deferred one.
Shafiis:	
a. The exchanged countervalues are all currencies or all foodstuffs and belong to the same genus, such as the sale of dates for dates or gold for gold.	No gain permitted in a hand-to-hand transaction and no deferred transaction permitted, even without gain.
b. The exchanged countervalues are all currencies or all foodstuffs but belong to different genera, such as the sale of gold for silver or dates for wheat.	No deferred transaction permitted even without gain. Gain permissible in a hand-to-hand transaction.

c. One of the exchanged countervalues is foodstuffs, the other is not, such as the sale of wheat for iron.	No deferred transaction permitted even without gain. Gain permissible in a hand-to-hand transaction.
d. The exchanged countervalues are neither foodstuffs nor currencies, whether or not they belong to the same genus, such as the sale of lime for lime or lime for lead.	Gain permissible whether in a hand-to-hand transaction or in a deferred one.
e. One of the exchanged countervalues is currency, the other is not, whether or not foodstuffs; examples are the sale of rice for silver or iron for gold.	Gain permissible whether in a hand-to-hand transaction or in a deferred one.

Hanbalis:

a. The exchanged countervalues are all measurable or all weighable and furthermore are foodstuffs, such as the sale of rice for rice, or grain for grain.	No gain permitted in a hand-to-hand transaction and no deferred transaction, even with no gain.
b. The exchanged countervalues are of the same genus and all foodstuffs but neither measurable nor weighable, such as the exchange of water-melons for apples, or all measurable or all weighable but not foodstuffs, such as the exchange of gold for silver.	Gain permissible in a hand-to-hand transaction but no deferred transaction permitted, even with no gain.
c. The exchanged countervalues belong to different genera and are properties governed by one *illa* i.e. they are all measurable or all weighable or all foodstuffs such as the sale of wheat for barley.	Gain permissible in a hand-to-hand transaction but no deferred transaction permitted, even with no gain.
d. One of the exchanged countervalues is currency and the other one an article susceptible to *riba*, i.e. measurable, weighable or foodstuffs.	Gain permissible in a hand-to-hand transaction and in a deferred one.
e. The exchanged countervalues belong to different genera and are governed by different *ilal*; for example, one is measurable (wheat), and the other is weighable (meat).	Gain permissible in a hand-to-hand transaction but conflicting opinion regarding deferment, with a trend towards permission.
f. The exchanged countervalues are all neither measurable nor weighable nor foodstuffs; an example is the sale of riding animals.	Gain permissible whether in a hand-to-hand transaction or in a deferred one.

The Malikis:	
a. The exchanged countervalues are all currencies or all storable nourishment for mankind and belong to the same genus as in the exchange of dinars for dinars or wheat for wheat.	No gain permissible in a hand-to-hand transaction and no deferred transaction even with no gain.
b. The exchanged countervalues are all currencies or all storable nourishment for mankind but belong to different genera, for example the exchange of dinars for dirhams or wheat for broad beans.	No deferred transaction permitted even with no gain. Gain permissible in a hand-to-hand transaction.
c. The exchanged countervalues are all foodstuffs which are not governed by the Maliki's illa whether or not they belong to the same genus, such as the sale of bananas for lettuce.	No deferred transaction permitted even with no gain. Gain permissible in a hand-to-hand transaction.
d. The exchanged countervalues are neither edible nor drinkable but are all either weighable or measurable, belong to the same genus and furthermore serve the same purpose, such as the sale of material for material.	No deferred transaction permitted even with no gain. Gain permissible in a hand-to-hand transaction.

Source: Saleh, 1986, pp20-26

The four *mazaheb* also differ in their opinions on whether Muslims are allowed to deal with *riba* with non-Muslims. Imam Abu Hanifa (699-767) allowed Muslims to enter non-Muslim territories and trade on the basis of *riba* (sale of one dirham for two). Abu Hanifa also allowed Muslims to trade on the similar basis with converted Muslims from non-Muslim countries. The Imamate of Shi'as is also of the opinion that as regards to transactions with non-Muslims, it is lawful for the Muslims to accept but not to give *riba*.

The Shafiis, Malikis and Hanbalis opposed the above opinion and believed that there should be no segregation in the prohibition of *riba*. They argued that since *riba* is prohibited in Muslim territories, therefore a similar rule should be applied in non-Muslim territories. Similarly, if it is unlawful for Muslims to accept or give *riba* to fellow Muslims, the same rule should be applied to transaction with non-Muslims.

3.5. The Views of Modern Muslim Scholars

One of the earliest controversial opinions pertaining to *riba* was given by Abdo (1849-1905), a Mufti of Egypt. Abdo was identified as a man with an open mind and sharp intellect. There was an allegation that Abdo issued a *'fatwa'* or 'ruling' that interest paid by the Post Office Savings Fund was not an element of *riba*. Rida (1865-1935), a student of Abdo, denied that the Mufti had issued such a *fatwa* but confirmed that certain Government officials, including the Director of Posts had a private discussion with the Mufti on this matter. *Al Manar*, an Egyptian magazine in its December 1903 issue, published a statement given by the Mufti on this matter. According to *Al Manar,* the Mufti had said *"The stipulated usury is not permissible in any case, whereas the Post Office invests the monies taken from the people, which are not taken as loans based on need. It would be possible to apply the investment of such monies on the rules of partnership in commendam"* (Homoud, 1985, p.122). This statement indeed created much controversy regarding its originality and validity. Rida also on many occasions expressed his opinion in matters relating to *riba*. One of the most controversial statements issued by Rida is that it is permissible for a person to borrow L. 100 and sign a note for L. 120 and this practice is not *riba*. According to Rida the deferred payment *riba* takes place upon the extension of debt upon maturity.

Dawalibi (1951), a prominent Muslim politician and journalist from Syria believed that reasonable interest should be allowed for loans of production. During the Scientific Conference of Islamic Jurisprudence which was held in Paris in 1951 he said, *"The banned usury takes place in loans meant for consumption not for production, where in the former sector the usurers take advantage of the need of the poor and destitute to exhaust them with exorbitant usury they impose on them. Nowadays, as the economic systems have been developed and many companies have been established, where most of the loans are being granted for production not for consumption, it is necessary to consider what development must be introduced to the stipulation's in consequence of this development of civilisation."* (Homoud, 1985. p.120). Discussion on the legality of *riba* during modern times was sealed off when The Council of Islamic Studies of The University of Al Azhar, Egypt, during its second conference, which was held in 1965, passed a recommendation that reaffirmed expressly and explicitly that interest on all kinds of loans was illegitimate *riba* and that much or little usury is illegitimate.

3.6 Summary

Muslims are prohibited from accepting or paying *riba*. This prohibition came from two main sources, the Quran and the *Hadith*. The prohibition in the Qur'an came via four revelations, whereas the Prophet (*pbuh*) on many occasions issued directives for Muslims not to deal in *riba*. The *riba* mentioned by the Qur'an is mainly known as *riba al-jahiliya* or pre-Islamic *riba*. This kind of *riba* was considered as a compensation to the creditors during pre-Islamic days who agreed to allow the debtors to defer their loan repayment. The *riba* which was mentioned by the Prophet (*pbuh*) is also known as sales *riba*. This *riba* can be further divided into two categories, increased *riba* and delayed payment *riba*. Increased *riba* is a *riba* which occurs when there is an inequality either in terms of quantity or quality in goods which are involved in a process of exchange. Delayed payment *riba* occurs when there is an increase in the 'countervalues' (value of the goods involved in the transaction) as a result of deferment of transaction.

There is no divergence in opinion among Muslims regarding the prohibition of *riba* in lending activities. *Riba*, however, is not committed in the case of an additional amount paid by the debtor over the principal sum if there is no expressed agreement which requires the debtors to do so. Difference in opinion, however, does occur in relation to sales *riba*. Similarly, there is no consensus of opinion among Muslims with regards to *riba* which occurred as a result of transaction between Muslims and non-Muslims. While Hanafis and Shi'ite allow their followers to deal on a *riba* basis, no such exemption is given to the followers of Shafiis, Malikis and Hanbalis.

References and Further Reading

Ahmad, Ziauddin (1992), 'The Theory of *Riba*.' in *An Introduction To Islamic Finance*, Sheikh Ghazali Sheikh Abod et. al.(ed), Kuala Lumpur, Quill Publisher, 1922, pp.56-69.

Al-Saud, Mahmud Abu (1992), 'Islamic View of Riba (Usury and Interest),' in *An Introduction to Islamic Finance*, Sheikh Ghazali Sheikh Abod et. al. (ed.), Kuala Lumpur, Quill Publications, pp.70-93

Ali, Abdullah Yusuf (1989*)*, *The Holy Qur'an: Text, Translation and Commentary*, Maryland, Amana Corporation.

Chapra, Muhammad Umar (1992), 'The Nature of Riba and its Treatment in the Quran, Hadith and Fiqh.' in *An Introduction to Islamic Finance*, Sheikh Ghazali Sheikh Abod et. al.(eds), Kuala Lumpur, Quill Publisher, 1992, pp.33-55.

Hitti, Philip K (1970). *Islam, A Way of Life*, Minnesota, University of Minnesota Press.

Homoud, Sami Hassan (1985), *Islamic Banking: The Adaptation of Banking Practice to Conform with Islamic Law*, London, Arabian Information Ltd.

Ismail, Abdul Halim (1992), 'The Deferred Contracts of Exchange in Qur'an.' in *An Introduction to Islamic Finance*, Sheikh Ghazali Sheikh Abod et. al.(ed.), Kuala Lumpur, Quill Publication, pp.284-313.

Khan, Mohsin S. (1987), 'Islamic Interest-Free Banking: A Theoretical Analysis.' in *Theoretical Studies in Islamic Banking and Finance*, Mohsin S. Khan and Abbas Mirakhor (eds), Houston, Institute for Research and Islamic Studies, pp.13-35.

Khan, Muhammad Muhsin (1986), *The Translation of The Meanings of Sahih Al-Bukhari.*, Vol III 6th. Edition, Lahore, Kazi Publications, 1986.

Manan, Muhammad Abdul (1986), *Islamic Economic: Theory and Practice*, Cambridge, Hodder and Stoughton.

Saleh, Nabil A. (1986), *Unlawful Gain and Legitimate Profit in Islamic Law: Riba, Gharar and Islamic Banking*, Cambridge, Cambridge University Press.

Chapter 4
Principle of *Shariah* in Islamic Banking

4.1 Introduction

Islamic banks in all countries are expected to conform to two types of laws. As normal business entities, Islamic banks are governed by laws and regulations imposed by the government of their domiciled country. These laws are commonly known as positive laws. As institutions whose foundations are based on Islamic doctrines, Islamic banks must also operate within the ambit of Islamic principles and laws. Without observing and following the foundations and rules as stipulated in the various sources of Islamic laws, no institution can claim itself as Islamic. Islamic laws are also known as *Shariah* laws.

Positive laws or the laws that are given by a person of authority are distinct from moral and sacred laws given by God or with God's guidance. These positive laws refer to Western laws and also to secular statutes borrowed by Islamic countries. The positive laws, in most cases are under the supervision of that country's Central Bank. In Malaysia for example, the establishment of Islamic banking is governed by The Companies Act (1965), and its operations are subjected to The Islamic Banking Act (1983). Islamic banks, therefore, must conform to all requirements as stipulated in both Acts. Similarly, other governments have passed special laws that govern the operations of Islamic banks in their country.

Schacht (1964) a contemporary historian in Islamic civilization, mentioned that Islamic law is an all-embracing body of religious duties, the totality of Allah's commands that regulate the life of every Muslim in all its aspects. It comprises, on an equal footing, ordinances regarding worship and ritual, as well as political and (in a narrow sense) legal rules. He believed that Islamic law was created not by an irrational process of continuous revelation but by a rational method of interpretation. Schacht also claimed that both religious standards and moral values which were introduced into the legal subject-matter provide the framework for a structural order.

Maududi (1983) argued that the main objectives of *Shariah* are to construct human life on the basis of *marufat* (virtues) and to cleanse it of the *munkarat* (vices). The term *marufat* denotes all the virtues and good qualities that have always been accepted as 'good' by human conscience. Conversely, *munkarat* denotes all the sins and evils that have always been condemned by human nature as 'evil'. In short, the *marufat* are in harmony with human nature and the *munkarat* are just the opposite. The *Shariah* gives a clear view of these *marufat* and *munkarat* and stresses these as the norms to which individuals and social behaviour must conform.

Besides highlighting the meaning of *Shariah*, this chapter will also elaborate on the sources of *Shariah* and its applicability to the Islamic banking system.

4.2 The Meaning and Concept of *Shariah*

The original meaning of word *Shariah* or *shar* is 'the path or the road leading to the water' and the verb *shara'a* literally means 'to chalk out or mark out a clear road to water.' In a religious sense, it means 'the highway of good life.' In other words, *Shariah* is the way which directs man's life to the right path (Rahman, 1979). From the words 'the right path' therefore, came the meaning 'law' (Denny, 1985). The word *Shariah* also has its correlation with the word *din* which literally means 'submission' or 'following.' *Shariah* is the ordination of the Way and its proper subject is God, whereas *din* is the following of that Way and its subject is man. Therefore, as far as Qur'anic idioms go, one may speak of *Shariah* and *din* interchangeably (Rahman, 1979).

The concept of *Shariah* is not only to govern man in the conduct of his life in order to realise the Divine Will, but covers all behaviour - spiritual, mental and physical. Therefore, *Shariah* principles are more than law, covering the total way of life that includes both faith and practices, personal behaviour, legal and social transactions. In other words, *Shariah* is a comprehensive principle of a total way of life.

Ismail (1992) in his elaboration on the root of Islamic banking and finance perceived Islam as comprising of three basic elements namely, *Aqidah*, *Shariah*, and *Akhlaq*. *Aqidah* concerns all aspects of faith and belief of a Muslim. *Shariah* as mentioned earlier is concerned with all forms of practical actions by a Muslim. *Akhlaq* covers all aspects of Muslim behaviour, attitude and work ethics with which he performs his practical actions. Aspects of *Shariah* can be further divided into two, namely *Ibadat* and *Muamalat*. *Ibadat* is concerned with the practicalities of a Muslim's worship of Allah, whereas *Muamalat* is concerned with the man-to-man relationship. Consequently, political, economic and social activities will be under the ambit of *Muamalat*. The Islamic banking system, therefore, being part of economic activities is linked to *Shariah* principles through *Muamalat*. The linkages between Islamic banking and the whole gamut of Islam are shown in Figure 4.1.

Figure 4.1
The Relationship Between the Banking System and Religion Within Islam

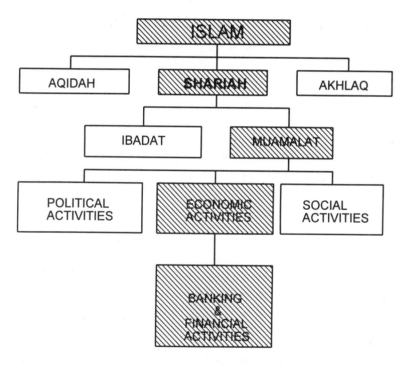

Source: Ismail (1992), page 250.

Ali (1950), nevertheless divided Islam into two parts namely, the theoretical and the practical. The theoretical aspects of Islam cover articles of faith or its doctrines and these aspects are known as *usul* (sing. *asl* which means 'a root' or 'a principle'). The practical aspects include all that a Muslim is required to do or, in other words, the practical course which he must conform. These practical aspects are known as *furu'* (sing. *far'* which means 'a branch'). The theoretical aspects are also called *aqa'id* (pl. of *aqidah*, lit. 'what one is bound to') or beliefs, while the practical aspects are also called *ahkam* (pl. of *hukm*, lit. 'an order') or ordinances and regulations of Islam. The existence of Islamic banking is therefore governed by the practical aspects of Islam and must therefore conform to the *ahkam* of Islam. There are five categories of *ahkam* or principles in *Shariah* law as described below.

1. *Fard* or *wajib*: Compulsory duties and acts to be performed by all Muslims. Performance is rewarded and omission is punished.
2. *Sunna, masnun, mandub,* or *mustahabb*: Duties and acts that are recommended but not required. Performance of them is rewarded, but omission is not punishable.
3. *Ja'iz* or *mubah*: Indifferent actions, whose performance or omission is neither rewarded nor punished.
4. *Makruh*: Actions that are disapproved but not punished or forbidden.
5. *Haram*: Actions that are both forbidden and punished.

Riba, for instance falls in the category of *haram* and is punishable.

4.3 Sources of *Shariah* Law

Basically, there are four fundamental sources of *Shariah* law. The first source is the Islamic Holy Book called Qur'an. The Holy Qur'an is the original and eternal source of *Shariah* law. It constitutes messages that *Allah* presented to the Prophet (*pbuh*) for the guidance of mankind. These messages are universal, eternal, and fundamental. The *Hadith*, the second foundation of *Shariah*, is next in importance to the Qur'an. It refers to information, accounts, narratives, stories and records of *Sunnah* of the Prophet (*pbuh*). These were handed down from generation to generation to become the rule of faith and practice of Muslims. The *Sunnah* (pl. *sunan*) signifies the customs, habits and usages of the Prophet (*pbuh*). It describes his behaviour, modes of action, his sayings and declarations under a variety of circumstances in life. The third source of *Shariah* law is the *Ijma*. *Ijma* means a consensus of opinion of *mujtahids* (learned scholars of Islam or those authorised to exercise independent legal reasoning), or an agreement of Muslim jurists of a particular age on a question of law. The fourth and last source of *Shariah* is the *Qiyas* which literally means 'measuring by' or 'comparing with' (Ali, 1950). *Qiyas* is the process of reasoning by anology of the *mujtahids* with regards to difficult and doubtful questions of doctrine or practice, by comparing them with similar cases already settled by the authority of the Qur'an and *Hadith* and thus arriving at solutions of undecided questions (Klein, 1985).

Both the Qur'an and the *Hadith* are called *al-adillat-al-qatiyyah* or absolutely sure arguments or infallible proof. This is because these sources contain absolute truth and the undoubted fundamental doctrines of Islam. The *Ijma* and *Qiyas* on the other hand are called *al-adillat-al-ijtihadiyyah* or arguments obtained by exertion. The former are also known as *usul* or the 'roots', whereas the latter are the *puruq* or the 'branches'.

Beside these four sources of *Shariah*, there are other minor sources such as *ijtihad* (to strive to the utmost), *ma'ruf* (well known or customary), *maslahat* (general good or welfare), and *istihsan* or *istislah* (public interest). The usage of these sources however, is often limited to certain schools of law. Sometimes these concepts are incorporated within the principles of *ijma* and *qiyas*.

4.3.1 The Qur'an

The Qur'an is the foundation of Islam and is primarily a book of religious and moral principles. It consists of one hundred and fourteen chapters of unequal length called *sura* (Sing. *surat*) which literally means 'eminence' or 'high degree' and each chapter has a special title. These chapters are further divided into verses called *ayah* (Sing. *ayat*) which means 'sign' or 'communication from God'. Without taking the 113 words of its opening verse (*Bismillah*) into consideration, the total number of verses is 6,240 (Ali, 1950). According to Doi (1984), the Qur'an contains 86,430 words, 323,760 letters of alphabet and 6,666 verses. The Qur'an also specifies as to whom, when, in what language, how, and why it was revealed. The Qur'an was revealed to the Prophet (*pbuh*) through a process called '*wahy matluww*' or 'revelation that is recited'. In this case, Gabriel or the Holy Spirit who acted as an intermediary gave directly to the Prophet (*pbuh*) Divine messsages from Allah.

Basically, chapters in the Qur'an are divided according to the place of revelation. Chapters revealed in Mecca are called the Mecca's chapters and those revealed in Medina are called the Medina's chapters. There are 92 Meccan chapters and the remainder was revealed during the Medina period (Ali, 1950).

To Muslims, the verses in the Qur'an belong to two intermingled portions namely, the portion which is the nucleus or foundation of the Book, and the portion which is figurative, metaphorical, or allegorical. The nucleus verses are also known as verses of 'established meaning' and are easily understood by ordinary Muslims. In the case of verses which have allegorical meanings, one who has well-versed knowledge in the science of interpretation or '*tafsir*' would be needed. The following are the pre-requisites before someone can interpret the Qur'an (Doi, 1984, p.35):

i.   Possess a sound and thorough knowledge of the Arabic language.

ii.   Be well-grounded in *ilm-al-maani* or knowledge of rhetoric.

iii. Have a sound and thorough knowledge of *Hadith* literature and science.

iv.   Should have an ability through the knowledge of the *Hadith*, to recognise that which is *mubham* (ambiguous) and to elaborate on that which is *mujmal* (brief or abridged).

v.   Have a sound knowledge of *asbab al-nuzul* (reasons for revelation) of the different verses from *Hadith*.

vi.   Have a thorough knowledge of *nasikh* and *mansukh* (abrogation of one verse by another).

vii. Possess good knowledge of *usul al-fiqh* (principles of Islamic jurisprudence).

viii. Possess good knowledge of *ilm al-tajwid* (the science of recitation of the Qur'an).

xi.   Be a man of *taqwa* (piety).

72

4.3.2 *Hadith*

Hadith literally means a story, a narration or a report (Rahman, 1979). It also has root meanings of 'being new' or 'occurring, taking place, coming to pass' and extends to talking about or reporting what has happened. Therefore, *Hadith* is a report of something that has taken place. This report or saying is conveyed to another party either through hearing or through revelation. *Hadith* is also known as 'tradition' because it was passed down from person to person and from generation to generation. In *Shariah*, *Hadith* describes the *sunnah* (the way or manner) of the Prophet (*pbuh*).

Sunnah literally means a way or rule or manner of acting or mode of life (Ali, 1950). The Qur'an also mentions the word *sunnah*. Rahman (1979) described the word *sunnah* as 'a trodden path' and each section of the path is considered as a *sunnah* regardless of its position or whether it is near to the starting point or remote from it. There are three kinds of *sunnah* (Ali, 1950):

a. A *qual* or a 'saying' of the Prophet (*pbuh*) which has a bearing on a religious question.

b. A *fi'l* which represent an 'action' or 'practice' of the Prophet (*pbuh*).

c. A *taqrir* or a 'silent approval' of the Prophet (*pbuh*) of the action or practice of another.

Hadith is the second and undoubted source from which the *Shariah* laws are drawn. This is in line with various verses in the Qur'an which commanded the believers to obey Allah and his Apostle (3:32; 4:59; and 59:7). As a source of *Shariah*, *Hadith* in many cases confirmed, extended, elaborated, explained, and complemented the revelation.

As far as the *Shariah* is concerned, not all the *Hadith* can be used as a source in formulating the law. *Hadith* in the category of *sahih* (sound) are the primary source of *Shariah*. The second category of *Hadith* is called *hasan* (fair) and *Hadith* in this category are not considered quite strong, but they are necessary for establishing a point of law. Indeed, most of the *Hadith* concerning legal matters are of this type. The last category of *Hadith* is *da'if* (weak) or *sakim* (infirm). *Hadith* which falls into this category deals with matters of law or with things which are allowable or forbidden will be rejected. For *Hadith* under the *sakim* category usage is considered only if it deals with exhortations, stories, and good behaviour.

4.3.3 Ijma

Ijma, or consensus, was originally the agreement of qualified legal scholars in a given generation and such consensus of opinion is deemed infallible. The emergence of this concept as a source of law is in line with the *Hadith* which says, " My community will never agree upon an error." This statement denotes the universal acceptance by all Muslims of the fundamental tenets of the faith, such as belief in the mission of Prophet (*pbuh*) and the divine nature of Qur'an. In its broadest sense, of course, *Ijma* is not the criterion of authority at all but simply the collected expression of a common religious conviction. *Ijma* was regarded as absolutely authoritative not only for discerning the right at present and the future, but also establishing the past: it was *Ijma* that determined what the *sunna* of the Prophet (*pbuh*) had been and indeed what was the right interpretation of the Qur'an. In the final analysis, therefore, both Qur'an and *Hadith* were authenticated through *Ijma* (Rahman, 1979).

The *Ijma* among the Muslim community is arrived at by *ijtihad* or exertion, or conscientious examination and meditation on the subject under consideration. Such consensus or agreement is generally said to be three fold:

a. Agreement of words or declaration of opinion in words.
b. Agreement of act or practice expresses in unanimity by action or practice.
c. Agreement of silence or tacit assent by silence or by non-interference.

Mujtahids (learned scholars) who are involved in this process must be men of integrity and honesty. Their minds must not be iniquitous (*fasik*) or blinded by passion (*hawa*) which inspire pernicious doctrines. There are three classes of *mujtahids* for this task namely, the absolute *mujtahid* who has absolute authority and whose sphere of exertion embraces the whole law, the *mujtahid* of a special school of theology who is an authority within the sphere of one of the special theological systems (*madzhab*) and lastly, *mujtahid* of special questions, and cases, which have not been decided by the founders of the four schools of laws (Klein, 1985).

4.3.4 Qiyas

The fourth source of *Shariah* is the *Qiyas*, which means literally 'measuring by' or 'comparing with', or 'judging by comparison' (Ali, 1950). Briefly it may be described as reasoning by analogy of *mujtahids*. Reasoning or the exercise of judgment, in theological as well as in legal matters, plays a vital part in Islam and the Qur'an clearly recognised this process. Verse 83 of Chapter 4, states:

> *"When there comes to them Some matter touching (Public) safety or fear, They divulge it. If they had only referred it To the Messenger or to those Charged with authority Among them, the proper Investigators would have Tested it from them (direct). Were it not for the Grace And Mercy of Allah unto you, All but a few of you Would have followed Satan."*

In Islam, those who do not use their reasoning faculty are compared to animals, and are spoken as being deaf, dumb and blind (2:171; 7:179; 8:22; and 25:44). While those who do not exercise reason or judgment are condemned and those who understand tend to be praised (190:3). The Prophet himself is reported to have sanctioned and encouraged the reasoning and the exerting of the faculties of one's mind, in order to find proper solutions for difficult and doubtful cases of law.

4.4 *Shariah* Laws in Islamic Banking System

As stated earlier, the objective of *Shariah* is to construct life on the basis of virtues and to cleanse it of vices. *Shariah* is, therefore, expected to provide not only the right path but also to govern all activities of the Muslims toward the betterment of the whole community. In reality, however, instead of being governed by the *Shariah*, Muslims are constantly bound by customary and positive laws. This situation which prevails in modern times commenced during the medieval age of Islam when the *Shariah* was frequently set aside by orders of the Caliph and governors, especially in matters related to commerce and civil order (Guillaume, 1977).

The emergence of Islamic banking in the 1960s and 1970s served as an impetus for the reestablishing of *Shariah* law in commercial activities. This was largely because banking laws in all Muslim countries were conventional banking laws or interest-based laws. But then interest is prohibited by the Qur'an and the *Hadith*. In order to allow Islamic banks to operate, governments of Muslim countries such as Pakistan and Malaysia commissioned Muslim jurists to promulgate laws which are applicable to this new style of banking. A similar approach was also taken at the international level. In December 1970, the second conference of Foreign Ministers of Islamic Countries commissioned a group of experts from 18 country members to study the proposal of establishing an International Islamic Bank for Trade and Development (Ali, 1988). This group in their submission, detailed the objectives and functions of the proposed institution, and also recommended the establishment of a consultative body in the field of Islamic banking and economics.

In the process of reestablishing *Shariah* law in banking, it was inevitable for Muslim jurists to refer to the primary source of *Shariah* i.e Qur'an and *Hadith*. The Qur'an, however, being primarily a book of religious and moral principles and exhortations is not a legal document. It nevertheless does embody important legal enunciations (Mannan, 1986). Khallaf (d.n.a.), has made the following classification of legal provisions found in the Qur'an (Zakaria, 1989):

1.	Source of law	: 50 verses
2.	Constitutional provisions	: 10 verses
3.	International law	: 25 verses
4.	Jurisdiction and procedures	: 13 verses
5.	Penal law	: 30 verses
6.	Civil law	: 70 verses
7.	Family and personal law	: 70 verses
8.	Economic and financial directives	: 20 verses

In regard to Islamic banking, the Qur'an has given clear and implicit guidelines that its operations should be free from any element of interest. As an ordinary business entity, the Islamic bank is expected to conform to the rules and guidelines given by the Qur'an. For example, Islamic banks are required by the Qur'an to fulfil their obligation towards their shareholders, depositors, partners, borrowers and other customers (2:177; 5:1; 16:91; 17:34). Islamic banks are expected to uphold trust, justice, and fairness in their dealings (4:58; 4:135; 5:8; 5:87; 6:152; 16:90; 17:35; 23:8; 55:8-9; 70:32-33). The Qur'an also provides guidelines for Islamic banks when dealing with those who borrow money from them (2:280 and 3:75). In terms of business procedures, the Qur'an prescribes details regarding the prosecution of contracts, and other covenants involved in the contract (2:282-283). Islamic banks are prohibited from investing in or to have any dealings with unproductive businesses (2:188) or businesses which promote obscenity, businesses which involve manufacturing, selling and transporting of liquor, making and selling of idols and services rendered in or to pagan places of worship, fortune-telling and drawing lots, and businesses that involve usury and bribery (2:188; 2:275-280; 3:130; 5:42; 5:90; 24:19) (Siddiqi, 1986).

There are also many *Hadiths* especially in the category of *sahih* which are very relevant and serve as guidelines to Islamic banking. Of foremost importance are *Hadiths* that prevent Muslims from associating themselves with the element of *riba*. Besides that, there are many other *Hadiths* in the area of sales, *as-salam* (sale in which price is paid for goods to be delivered later), renting, *al-hawala* (transfer of a debt from one person to another), representation, lending, payment of loans, freezing of property, bankruptcy, partnership, mortgaging, witnesses, and conditions of transactions. These *Hadiths* are consequently an important source of reference for Islamic banks in their daily operations.

Currently, there is no Muslim country which has succeeded in formulating and implementing a complete package of *Shariah* law which covers all aspects of living. Similarly Islamic banking laws are not comprehensive. In most cases the law is similar to conventional banking law except with an additional clause that prohibits the banks from dealing with interest. In the absence of well documented *Shariah* laws with regards to commercial transaction, Mahmasani (1982) believed that the concept of *Ijma* and *Qiyas* has become even more important in formulating new *Shariah* laws. These new laws are, however, confined to the field of *muamalat* (relationship between man to man) which includes commercial transactions, but have no value to *ibadat* or *i'tikadat* (worship).

77

4.5   Principles of *Shariah* in Islamic Banking

Muslim jurists and scholars have suggested a number of *Shariah* principles to be adopted by Islamic banks in delivering their products and services. Among the most widely used Sharia principles recommended by these scholars are *mudaraba, musharaka, murabaha, bai-mua'zzal, ijara, ijara wa-iktina, qard hassan, wadiah,* and *rahn.* Basically these principles can be broadly classified into four categories as below:

i.   Profit and loss sharing principles,
    a. *Mudaraba*
    b. *Musharaka*
ii. Fees or charges based principles,
    a. *Murabaha*
    b. *Bai mu'azzal*
    c. *Ijara*
    d. *Ijara wa-iktina*
iii. Free service principle,
    a. *Qard hassan*
iv. Ancillary principles.
    a. *Wadiah*
    b. *Rahn*

It is worth noting here that some scholars questioned the term 'profit and loss sharing' which was first used by the Council of Islamic Ideology of Pakistan in their report submitted to President Zia in 1980. These scholars urged that neither the entrepreneur nor the other suppliers of capital actually 'share' the loss accruing to any particular supplier of capital. In the case of *musharaka,* for example, each partner only shares the loss in proportion to their share in the financing, whereas the investor will bear all financial risks when *mudaraba* is used. Instead of 'profit and loss sharing', the term 'profit-sharing' was recommended by these scholars in referring to *musharaka* and *mudaraba* (Siddiqi, 1983). The term 'profit and loss sharing', however, is still widely used by Islamic banks in Pakistan and Bangladesh in describing the principles that govern their banking facilities. A similar approach is also taken by contemporary scholars (Khan and Mirakhor, 1987).

Besides the above principles, there are other isolated principles applicable to Islamic banking, but the usage of these principles is limited to specific Muslim countries. A brief explanation of the most widely used *Shariah* principles are as follows:

Mudaraba

Mudaraba means 'profit-sharing' or 'trust finance' or 'investment through self-employed entrepreneur'. This is basically an agreement between at least two parties, one being a lender or sometimes known as an investor and an entrepreneur also known as an agent-manager. In the agreement, the investor agrees to finance or entrust money to the entrepreneur who is to trade in an agreed manner and then return to the investor the principal and pre-agreed proportion of profits and keep for himself the remainder. The distribution of profit between two parties must necessarily be on a proportional basis and cannot be a lump sum or a guaranteed amount. In the case of loss as a result of circumtances beyond the control of entrepreneur, the investor will bear all financial risks and the entrepreneur loses the time and his efforts only.

Musharaka

Musharaka is normally translated in English as 'partnership'. In the context of Islamic banking, however, *musharaka* means 'participating financing'. Literally, *musharaka* means a joint-venture agreement between two parties to engage in a specific business activity with an aim of making profit. The termination of the agreement may be based on time or after fulfilment of certain conditions. In this principle, both parties will provide the capital and the investor or lender may also participate in the management. As in the case of *mudaraba*, all parties agree through negotiation on the ratio of distribution of profits generated from the business activity which need not coincide with the ratio of participation in the financing of the activity. However, in the event of loss, all parties bear the loss in proportion to their share in the financing.

Murabaha

Murabaha or 'cost-plus financing' or 'financing resale of goods' refers basically to the sale of goods at a price covering the purchase price plus a profit margin agreed upon by both parties concerned. This arrangement transforms a traditional lending activity into a sale and purchase agreement, under which the lender buys goods wanted by the borrower for resale to the borrower at a higher price, agreed upon by both parties. In this principle, Islamic banks play the same role as any other business entity i.e. giving services or sale of goods to customers with the aim of making profit.

Bai Mua'zzal

Bai-mua'zzal or 'deferred payment sale' is a variant concept of murabaha and in this case the borrower is allowed to defer settlement of payment for goods purchased within the period, and in a manner determined and agreed by both parties.

Ijara

This is the Shariah's concept of leasing finance, whereby the bank purchases the asset required by the customer, and then leases the asset to the customer for a given period. The lease, rental and other terms and conditions having been agreed upon by both parties.

Ijara wa-iktina

Ijara wa-iktina or 'lease purchase financing' refers to a contract where the bank purchases an asset for the purpose of renting the same to the customer against an agreed rental, together with the client's agreement to make payments which will eventually lead to the transfer of ownership from bank to customer.

Qard hassan

This is a benevolent loan that obliges a borrower to repay the lender the principal sum borrowed on maturity of the loan. The borrower, however has the discretion to reward the lender for his loan by paying any sum over and above the amount of the principal.

Wadiah

Wadiah or 'trusteeship' refers to an agreement between the owner of assets (excluding immovable fixed assets) and another party, whereby the owner will deposit and give consent to the custodian to make use of their assets (funds) as long as these assets remain in the custodian's hands.

Rahn

Rahn means pledge or pawn. It is a contract of pledging a security and becomes binding when possession of the pledge has taken place. In this principle the ownership of the security is not transferred to the pledgee. The transfer occurs only under certain conditions.

It is the consensus among Muslim scholars that the various principles adopted by Islamic banks belong to two categories: (i) strongly Islamic, and (ii) weakly Islamic. The principles can be considered 'strongly Islamic' if they conform to Islamic objectives both in form and in substance. 'Weakly Islamic' principles refer to practices which conform to Islamic norms in form but not in substance. The basis for judgement as to the strength or weakness of a given principle is the extent to which that mode contributes towards achievement of the objectives of Islamic economics (Islamic economics is a social science which studies the economic problems of people imbued with the values of Islam). Thus, only those principles which permit risk-return sharing between providers and users of funds can be considered strongly Islamic. Muslim scholars consider only two principles i.e. *mudaraba* and *musharaka* as strongly Islamic and the remaining principles are recommended only in cases where risk-return sharing cannot be implemented (Mirakhor, 1987).

4.6 The Usage of *Shariah* Principles by Islamic banks in Selected Muslim Countries.

A list of *Shariah* principles adopted by Islamic banking system of various Muslim countries is shown in Table 4.1. Except for the Islamic Republic of Iran, Pakistan and Sudan which have Islamised their entire banking system, other countries still maintain a dual banking system. Therefore, the *Shariah* principles highlighted in this Section are based on principles used by Islamic bank operating in those countries. In countries such as Malaysia, the Central Bank itself is responsible in determining the *Shariah* principles for Islamic banks or other financial institutions which intend to provide Islamic banking services.

Among the salient features in the application and elaboration of the *Shariah* principles by Islamic banks, the following are noteworthy:

i) The use of terminology,
ii) Category of principles,
iii) Number of principles,
iv) Country-specific principles.

4.6.1 The Use of Terminology

Malaysia is the only country where Arabic words are used in describing all *Shariah* principles governing Islamic bank operations. Other countries, however, retain Arabic words for certain principles only and use vernacular words for others. Some of the Arabic words which are commonly used by almost all Islamic banks are the principles of *mudaraba*, *musharaka*, *murabaha*, *ijara* and *qard hassan*. The slight differences in spelling are due to the variations in pronunciation of words in different countries.

With respect to terminology, two conditions have been observed. First, where the same practices are conducted but different terms applied. Second, where the same term is applied but different methods are practised. An example of the first condition is in the case of deferred payment. The principle of *bai-mua'zzal* is used by Islami Bank Bangladesh Limited (IBBL) of Bangladesh, but in Malaysia this principle is known as *bai bithaman ajil*. Similarly, the principle of instalment sales which is used by Islamic banks in Iran deals with deferred payment financing. The principle of *bai salam* of IBBL is a principle in which the bank will make an advance purchase and the customer will deliver the goods at a later date. This principle is similar to the principle of forward delivery which is used by Islamic banks in Iran. The principle of *bai al-dayn* used in Malaysia is for transactions involving sale and purchase of trade documents such as bill of exchange and bankers' acceptance. This principle is similar to the principle of debt purchasing practised in Iran.

An example of the second condition, that is, where the same term is applied but different methods are practised is in the case of *murabaha*. In Malaysia and Bangladesh, this principle covers mark-up transactions on a cash basis, whereas in the Middle East countries, the principle of *murabaha* covers both cash and deferred transactions. In the case of deferred transactions, some banks sometimes refer to this principle as *bai-murabaha*.

4.6.2 Category of Principles

Not all banks have adopted all the categories of *Shariah* principles which govern the banking operations. As stated in Section 4.5, there are four categories of *Shariah* principles, for banking namely, profit and loss sharing principles, fees or charges based principles, free services principles, and ancillary principles.

Except for IBBL of Bangladesh, Jordan Islamic Bank (JIB) of Jordan, Faisal Finance Institution (FFI) of Turkey, and the Islamic banking system in Malaysia which have adopted principles in all four categories, Islamic banks in other countries only employ three of the above mentioned four principles (see Table 4.1). Although these banks do not mention other ancillary principles such as *wadiah* (trust) and *rahn* (mortgage), in practice they too are involved in the activities which fall within the ambit of *wadiah* and *rahn*. For example, Bahrain Islamic Bahrain (BIB) of Bahrain, Kuwait Finance House (KFH) of Kuwait, Beit Ettamwill (BETS) of Tunisia, Dubai Islamic Bank (DIB) of the United Arab Emirates, and banks in Iran, Pakistan and Sudan provide mortgage based finance. Similarly current account facilities of banks in Pakistan, and KFH of Kuwait are based on *wadiah*.

4.6.3 Number of Principles

Within the four categories of principles there can be as many as 14 different principles employed by Islamic banks in their operations. Both BIB of Bahrain and DIB of the United Arab Emirates have the least number of principles i.e. five. The State Bank of Pakistan which is the central bank of Pakistan, has provided twelve principles to be used by all banks in Pakistan. Also in Iran, the Law for Usury-Free Banking 1983 has listed twelve principles.

Within the category of profit-loss sharing, except for Iran and Pakistan which have more than two principles, and BIB of Bahrain which has only one principle i.e. *musharaka*, other Islamic banks have two principles i.e. *musharaka* and *mudaraba*. Although it seems that Iran and Pakistan have more principles within the profit and loss category, these additional principles actually operate along the lines of both *musharaka* and *mudaraba*.

In the category of fees based principles, DIB of the United Arab Emirates has two principles followed by JIB of Jordan, with three principles. Malaysia which has only one full-pledge Islamic bank i.e. Bank Islam Malaysia Berhad (BIMB), has the highest number of principles i.e. nine, followed by Islamic banks in Pakistan which have seven principles. Principles in this category are used universally by all Islamic banks irrespective of countries. Principles within this category are further divided into three categories, namely, (i) fees based on mark-up, (ii) fees based on commission, and (iii) fees based on services. Products or services whose charges are based on mark-up are usually governed by the principle of *mudaraba, ijara, ijara wa-iktina (taajir* for Tunisia), hire-purchase, and *bai mua'zzal.* The marked-up amount is based on the nature of the transactions and the length of the credit given to the customer. Commission is usually received by Islamic banks for transactions based on the volume or amount. However, service charges are imposed on customers upon utilisation of bank services and the rate is fixed in line with the nature of services.

As for the free services category, all bank have adopted the principle known as *qard hassan.* Besides the Central Bank of Malaysia, three other banks (IBBL, JIB and FFI) have listed other principles which fall within the 'ancillary' category.

4.6.4 Country-specific Principles

Besides common principles (as explained in Section 4.5) some countries have specific *Shariah* principles for their Islamic banks. Although these principles are country specific, this does not necessarily mean that other countries are not familiar with those principles. While the other countries may apply these practices they do so by incorporating them into general banking rather than within specific *Shariah* principles. Generally, each Muslim country has its own religious body and is independent from one another. Therefore, it is the prerogative of the religious body within each country to establish its own principles and a particular principle adopted by specific country is not necessarily regarded as a distinct principle by other countries.

The principle of *bai-salam* which is applied in Bangladesh refers to a contract between buyer and a seller. The buyer gives an advance payment to seller based on a promise to deliver certain goods at a certain future date and place. Precise specifications of the quantity and quality of the goods are clearly mentioned in the agreement. The seller cannot deliver the goods before the date stipulated in the contract unless so agreed by the buyer. If the seller fails to deliver the goods on time, he is liable to return the advanced amount accepted previously from the buyer. Like the *bai-salam*, the principle of *istisna* which is available in

Kuwait also involves future delivery of goods. *Istisna,* however, refers to a contract between the buyer and manufacturer. Similar to the *bai-salam*'s contract, precise specifications of the quantity, quality, date and place of delivery must be outlined and agreed by both parties. Advance payment is not a prerequisite for a contract governed by the *istisna* principle in Kuwait.

In the case of Iran, for example, there are five additional principles within the profit-loss sharing category, namely, civil partnership, legal partnership, direct investment, *mozaarah* and *mosaqat*. While civil partnership, legal partnership and direct investment deal with the legal aspects of the formation of new ventures, both *mozaarah* and *mosaqat* are methods of agricultural financing.

The principle of civil partnership operates on the contribution of cash or non-cash capital by several persons or legal entities to a common pool on a joint-ownership basis, with the intention of making profit. This partnership will be terminated when the objectives of this partnership are accomplished. While civil partnership is common in the Western world, banks do not directly participate in them. Legal partnerships are created by the establishment of new joint-stock companies. In the case of direct investment, Iranian banks will make the investment or provide additional capital for productive projects. *Mozaraah* is a contract wherein one of the parties called *mozare* (bank) gives a specified plot of land for a specified period of time to another party called *amel* (contractor) for the purpose of farming and will divide the harvest between them according to an earlier agreed ratio. *Mosaqat* is a contract between the owner of trees (bank) and the like with another party in return for a specified common share of the produce. The produce can be fruits, leaves, flowers, etc.

Iran also has an additional principle called *jo'alah*. *Jo'alah* is the undertaking of one party *ja'el* or employer (either bank or customer) to pay a specified amount of money or wage to another party in return for rendering a specified service in accordance to the terms of the contract.

In the case of Pakistan, principles such as equity participation, participation terms certificate, *modaraba* certificate and rent sharing also operate on a profit-loss sharing concept. Equity participation involves the purchase of shares of companies by the bank. The bank will be treated as an ordinary shareholder of the company and will receive returns in the form of dividends. Participation term certificates are transferable financial instruments issued by a company for a specified period and are secured by a legal mortgage on the fixed assets of the company. A *modaraba* certificate is a certificate issued by companies which are registered under the *Modaraba* (Floating and Control) Ordinance of 1990. The returns on participation terms certificate and *modaraba* certificates are determined by the profitability of the issuing company. In the case of rent sharing, the bank provides finance for the building of houses, shopping complexes, flats, apartments, etc., and receives a share of the rental income of the property. In other countries, these activities are incorporated largely within the principles of *musharaka* and *mudaraba*.

Although Pakistan and Malaysia seem to have many *Shariah* principles for their fixed charges category, these principles can be grouped together within the principles of service charges. In Pakistan for example, development charges and service charges are terms used in imposing charges to customers. Similarly in Malaysia, the principles of *al-wakalah*, *al-kafalah*, *al-hiwalah*, and *al-ujr* are terms used by Islamic banking in Malaysia to represent the nature of services rendered to customers and how these charges will be imposed on customers.

The concept of *al-wakalah* (agency) which is used by Malaysia refers to a situation where a person nominates another person to act on his behalf. *Al-kafalah* (guarantee) refers to the guarantee provided by a person to the owner of goods, who has placed or deposited his goods with a third party, whereby any subsequent claim by the owner with regard to his goods must be met by the guarantor, and not by the third party. *Al-hiwalah* (remittance) refers to a transfer of funds/debt from the depositor's/debtor's account to the receiver's/creditor's account and, the concept of *al-ujr* (fee) refers to commissions or fees charged for services.

4.7 Summary

As institutions whose foundations are based on Islamic doctrines, Islamic banks must conform to Islamic rules and regulations. These rules and regulations are known as *Shariah* laws. *Shariah* can be divided into two basic components, *ibadat* (relationship between God and man) and *muamalat* (relationship between man and man). As a mechanism which mobilises material resources and being a part of economic activities, Islamic banking therefore, is governed by *Shariah* through the component of *muamalat*. The *Shariah* which governs the operations of Islamic banks comes from four sources, namely the Qur'an, *Hadith*, *Ijma* and *Qiyas*. While the Qur'an and *Hadith* are the primary source of *Shariah*, both *Ijma* and *Qiyas* are considered secondary and only applied when no solution on the matter in question is found in the Qur'an or *Hadith*.

Although various guidelines pertaining to business management are given in the Qur'an and *Hadith*, these guidelines are not properly codified and promulgated as complete rules and guidelines to be followed by Islamic banks thus making Ijma and Qiyas important. Since Islamic banking is comparatively new, no Muslim country has yet promulgated a complete set of *Shariah* laws to govern the entire Islamic banking system. In most cases the only *Shariah* component in Islamic banking law is the prohibition of interest in the operation of Islamic banks.

In the absence of interest, Muslim jurists have recommended various principles to be adopted by Islamic banks in delivering their products and services. These principles are broadly divided into four categories namely, profit-loss sharing, fees or charges based, free service, and ancillary principles. Both *mudaraba* and *musharaka* are considered profit-loss sharing principles, whereas principles such as *murabaha*, *bai-mua'zzal*, *ijara*, and *ijara wa-iktina* fall within the fees based category. While the principle of *qard hassan* is the only free service principle, *wadiah* and *rahn* are the principles in the ancillary category. Besides these common principles, there are other principles adopted by Islamic banks. The usage of these principles however, is country specific.

References and Further Reading

Ahmed, Osman (1990), 'Sudan: The Role of the Faisal Islamic Bank' in *Islamic Financial Market*, Rodney Wilson (ed), London (UK), New York (USA), Routledge, pp.76-99.

Ali, Maulana Muhammad, *The Religion of Islam, A Comprehensive Discussion of the Sources, Principles and Practices of Islam*, Lahore (Pakistan), The Ahmaddiyyah Anjuman Ishaat Islam.

Ali, Muazzam (1988), 'A Framework of Islamic Banking' in *Directory of Islamic Financial Institutions*, John R. Presley (ed), London (UK), Croom Helm, pp.3-13.

Table 4.1

List of *Shariah* Principles Practiced in Selected Islamic Countries

	Bahrain	Bangladesh	Iran	Jordan	Kuwait	Malaysia	Pakistan	Sudan	Tunisia	Turkey	UAE
(A)	Musharaka	Al-mudaraba Musharaka	Civil partnership Legal partnership Direct investment Modaraba Mozaarah Mosaqat	Mudaraba Musharaka	Mudaraba Musharaka	Al-mudharabah Al-musyarakah	Mushrika Equity participation and purchase of share Participation term certificate (PTC) Modarabah certificate Rent sharing	Mudaraba Musharaka	Mudharaba Musharka	Modaraba Mosharaka	Mudarabah Musharakat
(B)	Morabaha Commission Service charges	Bai-mua'zzal Bai-salam Hire-purchase Ijara Murabaha Commission Service charges	Forward delivery transaction Instalment sales Jo'alah Debt trading Hire-purchase	Murabaha Commission Service charges	Murabaha Commission Service charges Istisna Leasing	Al-murabahah Bai bithaman ajil Bai al-dayn Al-ijarah Al-ijarah thumma al-bai Al-wakalah Al-kafalah Al-hiwalah Al-ujr	Mark-up Purchase of trade bills Buy-back arrangement Leasing Hire-purchase Development charges Loan with service charges	Murabaha Ijara Commission Service charges	Murabaha Taajir Commission Service charges	Morabaha Ijara Ijara wa-iktina Commission Service charges	Murabahat Commission Service charges
(C)	Qard hassan	Quard-e-hassana	Qard al-hasanah	Al-qird al-hassan	Qard has-san	Al qardhul hasan	Qarz-e-hasna	Qard has-san	Interest free	Interest free	Qard hassan
(D)		Wadiah		Wadiah		Ar-rahn Al-wadiah yad dhamanah				Trust	

Source: IBB's 1994 annual report; Bangladesh: IBBL's CAD letter dated 21 March 1994, Iran: The Law for Usury-Free Banking 1983; Jordan: JIB's 1993 annual report; Kuwait: KFH's 1993 annual report; Malaysia: Money and Banking, Bank Negara Malaysia 1994; Pakistan: State Bank of Pakistan's BCD Circular no 13, 20th June 1984; Sudan: Ahmed, 1990; Tunisia: B.E.S.T Bank's 1992 annual report; Turkey: FFI's 1993 annual report; United Arab Emirates: DIB's 1992 annual report.

Notes:

(A) Profit and loss sharing principles,

(B) Fees or charges based principles,

(C) Free services principles,

(D) Ancillary principles.

Bank Negara Malaysia (1994), *Money and Banking in Malaysia*, Kuala Lumpur, Economics Dept, Bank Negara Malaysia.

Beit Ettamwill Tounsi Saudi (1992), *Annual Report*, Tunis (Tunisia).

Denny, Frederick Mathewson (1985), *An Introduction to Islam*, New York (USA), Macmillan Publishing Company.

Doi, Abdul Rahman (1984), *Shariah: The Islamic Law*, London (UK), Ta Ha Publishers.

Dubai Islamic Bank (1992), *Annual Report*, Dubai (The United Arab Emirates).

Faisal Finance Institutions (1993), *Annual Report*, Istanbul (Turkey).

Fyzee, Asaf A.A. (1974), *Outlines of Muhammadan Law*, 4th Edition, Delhi (India), Oxford University Press.

Guillaume, Alferd (1977), *Islam*, New York (USA), Penguin Books.

Islahi, Amin Ahsan (1989), *Islamic Law: Concept and Codification*, 2nd Edition, translated by S.A. Rauf, Lahore (Pakistan), Islamic Publications Ltd.

Islami Bank Bangladesh Limited (1994), *CAD Letter dated March 21*, Dhaka (Bangladesh).

Islamic Bank of Bahrain (1994), *Annual Report*, Manama (Bahrain).

Ismail, Abdul Halim (1992), 'Bank Islam Malaysia Berhad: Principles and Operations' in *An Introduction to Islamic Finance*, Sheikh Abod Sheikh Ghazali et. al. (eds), Kuala Lumpur (Malaysia), Quill Publications, pp.243-283.

Jordan Islamic Bank (1994), *Annual Report*, Amman (Jordan).

Khan, Mohsin S, and Abbas Mirakhor (1987), 'The Framework and Practice of Islamic Banking.' in *Theoretical Studies in Islamic Banking and Finance*, Mohsin S. Khan and Abbas Mirakhor (eds), Huston (USA), The Institute for Research and Islamic Studies, pp.1-13.

Klien, F.A. (1985), *The Religion of Islam*, London (UK) & Dublin (Ireland), Curzon Press Ltd.

Kuwait Finance House (1994), *Annual Report*, Safa (Kuwait).

Lewis Benard, V.L. Menage, Ch. pellat, and **J. Schachts** (eds) (1971), *The Encyclopedia of Islam*, New Edition, Leiden (Netherlands), E.J. Brill.

Mahmasani, Subhi, 'Adaptation of Islamic Jurisprudence to Modern Social Needs', in *Islam in Transition,* John J. Donohue and John L. Esposito (eds), New York (USA) & Oxford (UK), Oxford University Press, pp.181-187

Mannan, Muhammad Abdul (1986), *Islamic Economics: Theory and Practice (Foundations of Islamic Economics),* London (UK), Hodder and Stoughton.

Maududi, Abul Ala (1983), *Islamic law and Constitution,* Lahore (Pakistan), Islamic Publications Ltd.

Mirakhor, Abbas (1987), 'Short-term Asset Concentration and Islamic Banking' in *Theoretical Studies in Islamic Banking and Finance,* Mohsin S. Khan and Abbas Mirakhor (eds), Huston (USA), The Institute for Research and Islamic Studies, pp.185-199

Muslehuddin, Muhammad (1982), *Insurance and Islamic Law,* Delhi (India), Markazi Maktaba Islami.

Muslehuddin, Muhammad (1988), *Banking and Islamic Law,* 2nd Edition, Lahore (Pakistan), Islamic Publication Ltd.

Rahman, Fazlur (1989), *Islam,* 2nd Edition, Chicago (USA) & London (UK), The University of Chicago Press.

Schacht, Joseph (1964), *An Introduction to Islamic law,* Oxford (UK), Clarendon Press.

Schacht, Joseph (1979), *The Origin of Muhammadan Jurisprudence,* Oxford (UK), Clarendon Press.

Siddiqi, Nejatullah (1983), 'Comments on CII Report on Elimination of Interest' in *Money and Banking in Islam,* Ziauddin Ahmed, Munawar Iqbal and M. Fahim Khan (eds), Islamabad (Pakistan), Institute of Policy Studies, pp.223-232

Siddiqui, Muhammad Iqbal (1986), *Model of an Islamic Bank,* Lahore (Pakistan), Kazi Publications.

The Islamic Republic of Iran (1983), *The Law for Usury-Free Banking,* Tehran (Iran).

The State Bank of Pakistan (1984), *BCD Circular No 13, June 20,* Karachi (Pakistan).

Zakaria, Rafiq (1989), *The Struggle Within Islam,* New York (USA), Penguin Books.

Chapter 5
Deposit Facilities

5.1 Introduction

Like conventional banks, beside their own capital, Islamic banks are dependent on the depositors' money as a major source of funds. For conventional banks, deposit facilities cater to reasons of holding money. Following the Keynesian approach, people need money for three purposes: transaction, precaution and investment. Therefore, three categories of deposit facilities, demand, savings and time deposits are considered appropriate to fulfil these needs. Unlike conventional banks, there is no single approach adopted by Islamic banks in providing deposit facilities to their customers. In the case of the savings account for example, some banks consider this facility same with demand deposit facilities and others with time deposits. Consequently these banks do not provide any savings account facility to their customers. The users of deposit facilities of Islamic banks are individuals, business organisations and government bodies.

This chapter will elaborate various types of deposit facilities available at Islamic banks. The practice adopted by selected Islamic banks in delivering deposit services will also be highlighted.

5.2 Demand Deposits

For a conventional bank, a demand deposit facility is a deposit facility in which the owner is entitled to receive his or her funds on demand and to write cheques on the account, which transfers legal ownership of funds to others. This facility is widely known as current account and is designed for those who need money for transaction purposes. The purpose of using this facility is for convenience or to make payment for daily commitments. Seldom is interest paid on this account. In fact commercial banks in some countries besides charging the unavoidable cost such as the cost of the cheque book and stamp duty, will impose a moderate service fee on this account. There are, however, demand deposit facilities which provide returns to account holders. In the United States for example, commercial banks are allowed to provide the 'NOW Account (Negotiable Order of Withdrawal)' facility. NOW accounts are just demand deposits that pay interest. The banks, however, have the option to request seven days' notice prior to withdrawal of funds from these accounts. Similarly, in a country such as Malaysia, most commercial banks provide current account facilities that pay interest. There are, however, certain conditions to be fulfilled before account holders are entitled to receive interest.

Since this account can be devoid of the interest element, Islamic banks are permitted by *Shariah* to offer similar facilities. Generally, there are two *Shariah* principles, that is, *qard hassan* and *wadiah* which are used by Islamic banks in providing this facility. Islamic banks in some countries clearly indicate that they accept demand deposits based on the principle of *qard hassan*. The Law of Usury-Free Banking of 1983 of Iran, for instance specifies that current accounts of banks in Iran are operated on the *qard hassan* basis. Similarly, the Dubai Islamic Bank of the United Arab Emirates and the Kuwait Finance House of Kuwait, use the principle of *qard hassan* to govern their demand deposit facilities. Among Islamic banks which apply the principle of *wadiah* are banks in Bangladesh, Jordan and Malaysia. In Malaysia however, instead of *wadiah*, the principle is called *wadiah yad-dhamanah* or 'guaranteed custody'.

In Jordan, the demand deposit facility is known as the 'trust accounts' facility. The Jordan Islamic Bank for Finance and Investment Law No.13 of 1978 for example, states;

'Trust accounts are cash deposits received by the Bank where the Bank is authorised to use the deposits at its own risk and responsibility in respect of profit or loss, and which are not subject to any conditions for withdrawals or depositing.'

Trust accounts which are available at the Jordan Islamic Bank are further divided into two types of accounts called 'current' and 'demand'. Current account services offered by the Jordan Islamic Bank are basically the same as those offered by other Islamic and conventional banks. In the case of demand deposits, balances are represented by pass-books. Deposits and withdrawals are made upon presentation of the pass-book. In short, the Jordanian demand deposit is a current account without chequing facilities.

Chapter 5 – Deposit Facilities

Islamic banks in some countries do not indicate the types of *Shariah* principles that govern their demand deposit facilities. However, monetary authorities of some countries do issue rules and regulations pertaining to current accounts to be followed by Islamic banks. In the case of Turkey for example, the Undersecretariat of Treasury and Foreign Trade of the Prime Ministry issued the following rules and regulations (Presley, 1988):

Current Accounts

Article 15
It is an account to be opened in Turkish lira or in foreign exchange according to provisions to be set forth by Communiques and being payable partially or totally on demand; the account holder receives no interest, profit or other proceeds under whatever name they may be; the funds do not fall within the scope of the Savings Accounts Insurance Fund.

Specialities of Current Accounts

Article 16
Current accounts are booked and operated independently of Institution accounts and participation accounts and are booked and operated individually as Turkish lira accounts.

The Institutions transfers the profit and the loss incurred from the utilisation of funds accumulated in this account to its own accounts.

Current account creditors are first-priority creditors of the assets corresponding to current accounts as well as the capital and the reserve of the Institution for the total amount they have deposited.

The maximum amount the Institution can collect in its current account is determined by the Bank (The Central Bank of Turkey).

Utilisation of funds accumulated in Current Accounts

Article 17
A minimum of 10 per cent of the funds accumulated in these accounts shall be kept in cash or as deposits in commercial banks. An additional 10 per cent shall be kept in the bank either in cash or as liquid assets to be specified by the Bank. These percentages can be changed by the Bank.

The remainder of the funds can be utilised to finance commercial activities of real or legal persons, 50 per cent of which have a term of longer than one year. Eighty per cent of funds utilised shall be collected in cash when due and 20 per cent at the most can be participated to the profit and loss of the real or legal persons using the fund in accordance with the covenants of Contract for Profit and Loss Participation. The share the Institution receives from profit and loss, and, if necessary, the securities the Institution takes shall be clearly expressed in the Contract for Profit and Loss Participation investment.

The amount of a fund which can be associated with a single, real or legal person from these amounts shall be determined by the Bank.

Foreign exchange accumulated in these accounts can, furthermore, be utilised in Turkish banks and in international monetary and commercial markets.

Specific directives of the above mentioned nature are nevertheless rare. Such directives certainly assist in the understanding and operations of accounts. It must be noted that while the regulation is thorough with respect to procedure, there is no mention of the type of *Shariah* principle that is applicable for this variety of account.

Demand deposit facilities may be opened for various types of customers such as individuals, joint individuals, business organisations which include sole-proprietorship, partnership and companies, and other legal entities such as clubs, societies, and associations. There are a number of Islamic banks which provide current accounts in foreign currencies. Islamic banks in Turkey for example, provide current account facilities in both the US dollars and deutschmarks.

The following elements usually apply in the contract between Islamic banks and current account holders:

1. Money given to the bank will be considered as a loan if the principle of *qard hassan* is applied, but the money is given to the bank for safe custody when the *wadiah* principle is used.
2. If the deposit is made under the principle of *wadiah*, the bank seeks permission from customers to use these deposits at the bank's own risk as long as the funds remain with the bank. No permission is needed under the principle of *qard hassan*. No rewards will be given to customers.

3. The account holders may withdraw a part or whole of the deposits at any time they so desire, and the bank guarantees to honour such requests.

4. Both parties will abide by the rules and regulations related to the operational aspects of demand deposit accounts.

The common features of demand deposit facilities offered by Islamic banks are as follows:

1. This facility is available to parties who have the capacity to contract. In the case of an individual for example, only a person who has reached maturity age as stipulated by Islamic jurisprudence is allowed to maintain an account with the bank. Although the maturity age according to the majority of Muslims jurists is 12 years old, banks usually conform to the age established by common law and in most cases, no individual below 18 years old is permitted to open a current account. For business entities, clubs, societies, and associations, certificates of registration and documents such as memorandum and articles of association, minutes of meetings relating to the opening of an account must also be presented to the bank.

2. The bank uses its own discretion to determine the minimum balance required to open the account.

3. The bank will supply the account holders with a cheque book. Withdrawal from the account may be made on demand by issuing cheques or other written instructions given by the account holders. The cheques issued by customers will be honoured by the banks subject to the conditions that they are in order and funds are available in the account. The cheque will also be returned by the bank for technical reasons such as difference in signature, post-dated or out-of-date and invalid amendments.

4. A service charge may be imposed by the bank for servicing and maintaining the account. A penalty may be imposed for any cheque returned due to an insufficient balance in the account.

5. The termination of the relationship between the bank and account holders can be effected either upon the customer's request or at the discretion of the bank. Due notice of such intention must, however, be given by the intended party. The ac-

count will also be suspended in the case of death or bankruptcy of individual customers and winding up of a company or other legal instruction such as orders from the court.

There is, therefore, little difference between the operational procedures of demand deposit facilities of conventional and Islamic banks. Although no reward is given to current account holders by most Islamic banks, Islamic banks in Iran are allowed to reward their customers. As stated in the Law for Usury-Free Banking of 1983 of Iran, Islamic banks are permitted to give a non-fixed bonus in cash or in kind to *qard hassan* deposits. In Malaysia, Bank Islam at its own discretion, provides rewards to accounts maintained by Federal and State Government and Statutory Authorities provided that they maintain a minimum daily balance of not less than RM25,000.00.

5.3 Savings Account
The second category of deposits is the savings account. To conventional banks, this account is to facilitate those who wish to save money and at the same time to earn an income. The depositors in this category are those who hold money primarily because of precautionary motive while simultaneously induced by an investment motive.

Except for Islamic banks in Turkey, Islamic banks in other countries do provide savings account facilities. There is no standardisation among Islamic banks in providing this facility to customers. Various *Shariah* principles are used to govern this facility. Not all savings account customers receive returns from their deposits.

The three *Shariah* principles used by Islamic banks for savings account are *qard hassan*, *wadiah* and *mudaraba*. Like current accounts, savings account facilities of banks in Iran are governed by the principle of *qard hassan*. In the case of the Faisal Islamic Bank of Bahrain, the principle of *wadiah* is applied for both current and saving accounts. Similarly, the principle of *wadiah yad-dhamanah* is used by banks in Malaysia. However, the majority of Islamic banks prefer to use the principle of *mudaraba*. The Kuwait Finance House of Kuwait is the only Islamic bank which has clearly indicated that both the principles of *qard hassan* and *mudaraba* are applicable for its savings account facility. In this case only a certain portion of funds in the savings account is used for investment purposes and depositors will be rewarded based on that portion. At Dubai Islamic Bank and the Islamic Bank Bangladesh, all funds deposited in savings accounts are invested in various business activities. This means that returns to depositors are calculated based on the total funds placed in the account.

Among Islamic banks which do not provide any return to their savings account holders are the Faysal Islamic Bank of Bahrain and the Faisal Islamic Bank of Sudan. At the Faysal Islamic Bank of Bahrain, the savings account is treated as another form of current account except that deposits and withdrawals are made upon presentation of the passbook. This facility is made available for small savers who do not require chequing facilities.

Although the principle of *qard hassan* is used by banks in Iran and the principle of *wadiah yad-dhamanah* is used by banks in Malaysia, and under these principles customers are not entitled for any kind of reward, banks in these two countries, nevertheless do provide rewards to their savings account customers. In Iran, the rewards given by banks could be in the form of cash or other goods such as air tickets to holy shrines, carpets, gold coins and cars. The savings account customers can also get exemption or reduction from payment of commission for utilising banking services (Aryan, 1990). In Malaysia, the reward for saving account holders is usually in the form of rates of profit announced by the bank on a monthly basis.

Some Muslim scholars argue the lawfulness of the practice of rewarding savings account customers that operate via principles other than *mudaraba*. Ariff and Mannan (1990) for example, questioned the procedures relating to savings accounts adopted by Bank Islam Malaysia and argued that rewards to savings account holders if done on a regular basis is a form of *riba*. A similar position was taken by the *Shariah* Supervisory Board of the Faisal Islamic Bank of Sudan. This Board had issued a *fatwa* which suggests that it is permissible to give prizes for savings accounts without prior knowledge of its holders so long as the prizes are varied and made on a non-regular basis (Salama, 1990).

When the principle of *mudaraba* is applied, the bank becomes an entrepreneur or '*mudarib*' and the savings account customers become investors or '*sahib al-maal*'. Banks then employ the deposited funds into various business activities and share any profit with depositors based on a pre-agreed ratio. In the case of loss, the entire loss will be borne by depositors.

Like current accounts, various elements of contracts are applied between the bank and the savings account holders. These elements include specification on the type of contract between the bank and the customer, procedures relating to deposits and withdrawals, and regarding rewards distributed to customers. Similarly, some of the features imposed upon current account facilities are applicable to savings accounts. For example, the bank is entitled to establish a minimum balance of deposit required to open an account, the types of customers acceptable and other operational procedures. A minor is sometimes allowed to open a savings account with the bank but the account is opened in the name of his or her parent or guardian. The following procedures adopted by Islami Bank Bangladesh which is fairly typical of all Islamic banks is given below (IBBL, 1994):

PLS-Savings

1. Any individual singly or jointly and any socio-economic institution can open this account by tendering an initial deposit of Tk.100 (Taka one hundred) only.

2. Withdrawal is ordinarily allowed 4 (four) times in a calendar month up to 25 per cent of the balance or Tk.15,000 (Taka fifteen thousand) whichever is less in a single transaction.

3. For withdrawal of amount exceeding the above limit, 7 (seven) days' prior notice is required, otherwise no profit is allowed for that month.

4. For the purpose of calculation of profit, the lowest balance standing in the account from 6th to the last day of that month is taken into consideration. Profit is credited to accounts provisionally in June and December every year. Final rates of profit are declared after closing of accounts in December and auditing of the same by the Statutory Auditors. The amount of provisional profit credited in June and December is adjusted on the basis of the final rate.

5. The PLS-Savings account can be operated by cheque.

6. Collection of bills, cheques and other negotiable instruments is undertaken on a limited scale.

Although some Islamic banks adopt similar principle i.e. *mudaraba* for savings account facility, there is no single approach for calculating returns to depositors. The Dubai Islamic Bank, for example, adopts the following approach (DIB, undated):

> "The profit in the savings account are calculated on the minimum balance during the month. The account holder is given profit according to the common percentage of profits. The profits are distributed at the end of every financial year after the approval of the Bank's balance sheet by the General Association. The depositor in the Savings Investment Account participates in the profit of the Savings Investment w.e.f. the beginning of the following month after the month during which the deposit took place. The profits are not calculated w.e.f. the beginning of any month during which the money is withdrawn from the account. The minimum balance for considering the profit is Dh.1000 (Dirham one thousand)."

In the case of the Bank Islam Malaysia, although the principle of *wadiah* is in used, this Bank nevertheless has a standard formula for calculating rewards for savings account holders. In the case where the bank decided to reward the savings account holders, the amount of profit distributed to customers is calculated based on the following formula:

$$MP = \frac{\text{CDB for the month}}{\text{Number of days in the month}} \times R \times \frac{1}{12}$$

Where,

MP : Profit for the month
CDB : Cumulative daily balance in the savings account
R : Rate of profit given at the end of month.

The above formula is used with the assumption that profit is distributed on a monthly basis. However, no mention is made on how rate of profit (R) is determined.

5.4 Investment Deposits

The third category of deposit facility is for those who keep money for investment motives. Customers who have idle funds usually want better returns. These customers, normally prefer to place their money in the time (fixed) deposit facilities. In the Islamic banking system, this facility is called 'investment deposit'. All investment deposits available at Islamic banks are governed by the principle of *mudaraba*. Within this context, Islamic banks act as entrepreneurs or managers and depositors become investors. The bank would provide no guarantee or no fixed return on the amount deposited and under the principle of *mudaraba*, the customer will share the profits or losses made by the bank. The agreement on how the profit or loss will be distributed between the bank and the depositor is made at the beginning of the deposit and cannot be amended during the tenure of the deposits, except by consent of both parties.

There are a few alternatives available within this type of deposit as highlighted below:

1. Deposits based on duration.
2. Deposits based on notice.
3. Deposit for a specific project or purpose.

Investment deposit facilities based on duration are available at all Islamic banks in all countries. Under this arrangement, customers are free to chose the period that they want to place their funds with the bank. The common arrangement of this kind of deposit is on quarterly basis i.e. 3 months, 6 months, 9 months, one year or more. Some Islamic banks do provide investment deposit facilities on a monthly basis. The minimum amount required for this arrangement is usually higher than deposits for a longer period. In Malaysia, for example, a minimum deposit of RM5,000 is required to open an investment account for a period of one a month, whereas RM500 is sufficient for other types of investment accounts. Unlike other banks in which investment deposits are based on a quarterly basis, both the Jordan Islamic Bank and the Kuwait Finance House offer investment deposits on a yearly basis only and the minimum duration of any deposit is for a period of one year.

Unlike the Jordan Islamic Bank which provides investment deposit facilities for a period not less than a year, customers at the Kuwait Finance House are however given two options: (i) investment deposits to be placed for a limited period, and (ii) investment deposits for an unlimited period. Investment deposits for a limited period are valid for one year and renewable only by specific instructions from depositors. In the case of investment deposits for an unlimited period, the withdrawal is made on a yearly basis. Although the duration of deposit is unlimited, customers are allowed to withdraw their deposits after a one year period. Three months written notice is required prior to any withdrawal and without such notice the deposit is automatically renewed.

Investment deposit facilities based on notice are only available at the Islami Bank Bangladesh and the Jordan Islamic Bank. This deposit facility differs from other deposits based on duration since depositors are not allowed to withdraw their deposits without submitting a notice prior to withdrawal. Customers of Islami Bank Bangladesh must give seven days' notice and ninety days' notice is required at the Jordan Islamic Bank.

Investment deposits for specific projects or purposes are available at selected Islamic banks and on a limited scale. In this kind of deposit the depositor agrees to invest in a particular project selected by him/her. The profit of the particular project is distributed between the bank and the customer according to mutually pre-agreed terms and conditions.

Like current and savings accounts, there are a few common features adopted by Islamic banks when providing investment deposit facilities. Among these features include stipulations on minimum amount of deposit, types of customers who can operate an investment account, withdrawal and renewal process and distribution of profits. In most cases, depositors are not allowed to withdraw their deposits fully or partially before the maturity date. When withdrawal is allowed depositors will not be entitled to any profit.

As mentioned earlier, the Kuwait Finance House (KFH) has two types of investment deposit facilities, investment deposit for limited as well as for unlimited periods. Except for the maturity period and renewal process, similar procedures are applied for both deposit facilities. Both facilities require a minimum deposit amount of KD1,000 (Kuwaiti Dinars one thousand). The returns (profit) for these deposits is payable at the end of the fiscal year and according to the realised profit and the percentage determined by the bank. Other operational procedures of the KFH investment deposit facility are as follows (KFH, 1977):

1. KFH will issue a deposit certificate in the name of the depositor for the deposited amount.
2. The depositor or the beneficiary or whoever has the right to withdraw, cannot withdraw any part of the deposit before the due date.

3. The investment of the deposit is carried out on the basis of absolute speculation and KFH have a free hand to invest it in the way seen proper for realising mutual advantage.

4. The depositor or beneficiary or whoever is authorised to withdraw the deposited amount, can withdraw the deposit on the due date against presentation of the deposit certificate to KFH and after signing the final settlement.

5. The beneficiary may abdicate or negotiate the deposit certificate to another party on the same conditions agreed upon with the KFH provided that he turns up at KFH premises and presents the deposit certificate to record the abdication in the KFH registers and in replacement of the old certificate KFH will issue a new certificate in the name of the new beneficiary.

6. In case the certificate happens to be damaged or lost KFH must be notified forthwith to take necessary precautions at the client's expense and to re-issue a substitute certificate exempting KFH from any responsibility whatsoever.

7. The return (profit) of the deposit will be paid periodically as determined by the administration of KFH.

8. The certificate should be stamped by KFH bearing two signatures of two officials authorised to sign in this respect.

As seen from the above description of operational procedures of Islamic investment deposits facilities are not too different from the procedures of term deposits available at the conventional banks.

Islamic banks in most countries are free to establish their own investment account's operational procedures. In the case of Islamic banks in Turkey, however, the details of operational procedures for investment accounts (called participation accounts in Turkey) are given by the Undersecretariat of Treasure and Foreign Trade (known as Communique of Under secretariat of Treasure and Foreign Trade). The procedures given by this body cover specific features of investment accounts (Article 19), utilisation of funds accumulated in the accounts (Article 20), early withdrawal (Article 21), depositing (Article 22), and closing of accounts (Article 23).

The utilisation of funds accumulated in 'participating accounts' as described by Article 20 of the Communique are as follows (Presley, 1988 p.338):

a. An amount to be determined by the Bank not in excess of 50 per cent of those amounts retained in the Bank as per Article 17, paragraph 1, shall be blocked in the Bank as per provisions set forth in the said article.

b. The non-blocked funds may be allocated to the use of real and legal persons in the following manners:

Production assistance

This will be realised through buying the necessary goods and equipment and real estate from third parties in cash and selling these on credit to those who apply for the provision of real estate, raw or semi-finished material and machinery and equipment for their enterprises. The finance house is required to complete the purchase and sale contracts simultaneously in accordance with the freedom of entry into contracts.

Utilisation of funds by participation in profit and loss

In order to place the participation funds in profit and loss, the Institution shall sign a 'Contract for Profit and Loss Participation Investment' with real and legal persons who will use these funds. Participation in profit and loss can either cover all activities or only one activity of the fund-user of the profit and loss resulting from buying and selling of a specified amount of goods. The Institution can have a claim on the profits at a ratio specified in the Contract of real and legal persons using these funds; in the case of loss, the Institution participates in the loss according to the maximum amount allocated for that activity.

Rental contract (leasing)

This is the leasing equipment to be utilised in the production of goods and services to enterprises while retaining the title of such equipment in the Institution.

Placement of funds upon documentary letters of credit

This type of placement is relevant only for activities permitted by the Foreign Trade Regulation.

A contract is signed between the House and the fund-user which regulates purchasing of the document by the Institution

in cash and reselling it to the fund-user at a higher price on
credit.

c. Funds not utilised in the ways specified above can be kept i n
banks.

d. The Institution is required to allocate, starting from the second
year of activity, a minimum of 25 per cent of the funds accumulated in Participating Accounts to activities earning foreign exchange.

e. The Bank determines the maximum amount of funds which will
be used by a single real or legal person from the funds accumulated in each pool.

This shows that Islamic banks in Turkey are stringently monitored
by government authorities possibly to grant greater security and stability
to the financial system.

5.5   Other Deposit Facilities

Other types of deposits facilities have not fully developed in the Islamic
banking system. For instance, 'Negotiable Certificate of Deposits
(NCD)' and 'Negotiable Order of Withdrawal (NOW)' facilities available at conventional banks are not available at Islamic banks. Islamic
banks in some countries, however, are allowed to introduced deposit
facilities other than facilities which fall into the categories of current,
savings and investment account facilities. For example, the Jordan Islamic Bank has been allowed to introduce the *muqaradah* bond to be
sold to the public so as to tap the savings. Similarly, financial institutions in Malaysia which participate in Islamic banking are allowed to
provide *al-mudharabah* Interbank Investment (MII) facilities. While the
muqaradah bond facility has not been fully explored by the Jordan Islamic Bank, the *mudharabah* interbank investment facility is only available for participants in the Malaysian Islamic financial market.

5.6   The Structure of Deposit Facilities at Islamic Banks in
Selected Islamic Countries

The structure of deposit facilities available at Islamic banks and in selected Islamic countries is listed in Table 5.1. Some of the similarities
and differences in terms of deposit facilities are highlighted below:

1. Accounts which operate on the *mudaraba* principle are the most well received deposits facilities among the customers of Islamic banks. In the case of IBB of Bahrain for example, at the end of 1994, the total funds provided by these facilities was 90% of the total deposits. Turkey had a similar percentage. El Gharb of Sudan has the lowest percentage for this kind of account, that is, 10% of total deposits.

2. Savings accounts facilities operating on a *mudaraba* principle is more attractive to depositors as compared to investment account facilities (all investment accounts operate on the *mudaraba* principle). At MCB of Pakistan, for example, the percentage of savings accounts was 45% and investment accounts only 24% of total deposits. At IBBL Bangladesh, it was 45% against 36% respectively. And 58% and 26% for KFH of Kuwait. JIB of Jordan is the only bank which differed from this trend with savings accounts of 8% and 71% of investment accounts relative to total deposits.

3. The percentage of savings accounts (relative to total deposits) operating on principles other than *mudaraba* is smaller, not only to the percentage of current accounts, but also to savings accounts which operate on *mudaraba*. For example, the percentage of savings accounts of BIMB of Malaysia which operate under the principle of *wadiah yad-dhamanah* is 15% of its total deposits and the percentage of current accounts is higher i.e. 17% of total deposits. BMI of Iran has the smallest percentage of savings accounts i.e 5% of the total deposits and this account is governed by the principle of *qard hassan*.

4. Current accounts are also major providers of funds to the Islamic banks, more so for Islamic banks in Sudan. At the El Gharb of Sudan for example, at the end of 1993 the current accounts constituted 57% of total deposits. BMI of Iran also has a high percentage of current accounts as compared to other deposit facilities i.e. 34%. For other banks, only about 20% of total deposits are placed in the current accounts. The banks where funds deposited in current accounts is 10% or less of total deposits are FFI of Turkey and BIB of Bahrain.

5. Both current and investment accounts facilities using foreign currencies have received a tremendous response from customers in Turkey. At the end of 1993, these accounts constituted 85% of the total deposits placed by customers at FFI of Turkey. Other banks do not indicate the size of foreign currency accounts in their annual reports.

6. BIMB of Malaysia is the only bank where the figure for 'other deposits' facility was higher than current and savings accounts figures. The clients who deposit into this facility are mainly government agencies. Usually the terms for this deposit are subject to negotiations between the bank and the depositor. Similarly at El Gharb of Sudan, the figure for this facility was higher than savings and investment accounts. In Sudan however, the bulk of this deposit is mainly from marginal deposits required by the Bank prior to the issuance of letters of credit.

5.7 Summary

Like conventional banks, there are three types of deposit facilities available at Islamic banks. The first type of deposit can be regarded as equivalent to demand deposit at conventional banks. Depositors are allowed to withdraw their funds at any time without any notice. In most cases, Islamic banks would guarantee to return the deposited amount. Also no return is paid on this type of deposit. Islamic banks may impose service charges on this deposit. Generally, there are two Shariah principles, that is, *qard hassan* and *wadiah* used by Islamic banks in providing this facility.

The second type of deposit facility is the savings account. To conventional banks, this account is to facilitate those who wish to save money and at the same time earn an income. Depositors in this category are those who hold money primarily for precautionary motives and are simultaneously induced by investment motives. Except for Islamic banks in Turkey, banks in other countries do provide savings account facilities. Unlike savings accounts with conventional banks where the depositors receive interest on their deposits, not all Islamic banks reward their savings account customers. Three widely used *Shariah* principles governing this facility are *qard hassan*, *wadiah* and *mudaraba*.

Table 5.1
The Structure Deposit Facilities of Islamic Banks in Selected Countries

B'rain	%	B'desh	%	Iran	%	Jordan	%	Kuwait	%	M'sia	%	P'tan	%	Sudan	%	Tunisia	%	Turkey	%	UAE	%
CA	10	CA & ConA	19	QH CA	34	TrA	20	CA	14	CA	17	CA & ConA	20	CA	57	CA	11	CA:		CA	21
IA:		PLS:		QH SA	5	JIA:		IA:		SA	15	PLS:		SA	2	SA	13	Turkish	4	SA	18
SA	33	SA	45	ID	52	SA	8	SA	58	IA	50	SA	45	ID	10	ID:		Foreign	6	IA	59
TD	57	TD	32	IBD	9	F & NA	71	LP	*	IBD	*	TD	24	OD	31	UD	49	PLS:		IBD	1
		SND	4			IBD	1	UP	26	OD	18	IBD	11			CD	27	Turkish	11	OA	1
								IBD	2									Foreign	79		
Total	100	Total	100	Total	100	Total	100	Total	100	Total	100	Total	100	Total	100	Total	100	Total	100	Total	100
% TL	92	% TL	80	% TL	92	% TL	81	% TL	85	% TL	87	% TL	98	% TL	59	% TL	74	% TL	89	% TL	83

Notes:

1. QH: Qard hassan, CA: Current accounts, SA: Savings account, ID: Investment deposits, IBD: Inter-bank deposits, OD: Other deposits, ConA: Contingency accounts, TD: Term deposits, SND: Short notice deposits, IA: Investment accounts, LP: Limited period, UP: Unlimited period, TrA: Trust accounts, F & NA: Fixed & notice accounts, UD: Uncommitted deposits, CD: Committed deposits, TL: Total liabilities.

2. * Less than 0.5 per cent.

3. Contingency accounts which are available at MCB of Pakistan and IBBL and IBBL of Bangladesh comprise of marginal deposits placed by customers for using facilities such as letters of credit and bank guarantees.

Source: Bahrain: IBB's 1994 annual report; Bangladesh: IBBL's 1993 annual report; Iran: BMI's 1992 annual report; Jordan: JIB's 1993 annual report; Kuwait: KFH's 1993 annual report; Malaysia: BIMB's 1994 annual report; Pakistan: MCB's 1993 annual report; Sudan: El Gharb's 1993 annual report; Tunisia: BETS's 1992 annual report; Turkey: FFI's 1993 annual report; United Arab Emirates: DIB's 1992 annual report.

The third type of deposit facility available to customers is investment deposit and this facility is governed by the principle of *mudaraba*. Within this context, the Islamic bank will act as an entrepreneur or an agent-manager and the depositor as an investor. There are a few alternatives available within this type of deposits, namely, deposits based on duration, notice, and for specific projects or purposes. The bank would provide no guarantee, nor fixed return on the amount deposited and under the principle of *mudaraba*, the customer will share the profits made by the bank. The agreement on how the profit will be distributed is made at the beginning of the term and cannot be amended during the tenure of the deposit, except by consent of both parties. In the case of loss, the entire amount will be borne by the depositor. The distribution of profits for depositors may be on a quarterly, half-yearly, or yearly basis and withdrawal before maturity is usually prohibited. In the case of early withdrawal, the depositors would not be eligible to any profit.

Other deposit facilities such as 'Negotiable Order of Withdrawal' and 'Negotiable Certificate of Deposits' have not been developed by Islamic banks. There are however steps taken by Islamic banks in some countries to provide other deposits facilities to customers. In Jordan, for example, the Jordan Islamic Bank has been allowed to issue bonds based on Islamic principle called '*al-muqaradah*'. Similarly, banks in Malaysia are allowed to issue Islamic investment certificates. The issuance of these certificates, however, is limited to the participants in the Islamic inter-bank market.

References and Further Reading

Ariff, Mohamed and M.A. Mannan, eds (1990), *Developing a System of Financial Instruments*, Jeddah (Saudi Arabia), IRTI, Islamic Development Bank.

Aryan, Hossein (1990), 'Iran: The Impact of Islamization on the Financial System' in *Islamic Financial Market*, Rodney Wilson (ed), London (UK) and New York (USA), Routledge, pp.155-170.

Bank Islam Malaysia Berhad (1992), *Notes distributed during the seminar on Islamic Banking organised by IBBM*, Kuala Lumpur (Malaysia).

Bank Islam Malaysia Berhad (1994), *Annual Report*, Kuala Lumpur (Malaysia).

Bank Melli of Iran (1992), *Annual Report*, Tehran (Iran).

Bank Negara Malaysia (1994), *Money and Banking in Malaysia*, Kuala Lumpur (Malaysia), Economic Department, BNM.

Beit Ettamwill Tounsi Saudi (1992), *Annual Report*, Tunis (Tunisia).

Dubai Islamic Bank (1992), *Annual Report*, Dubai (U.A.E.).

Dubai Islamic Bank (undated), *Information Leaflet*, Dubai (U.A.E.).

El Gharb Bank of Sudan (1993), *Annual Report*, Khartoum (Sudan).

Faisal Finance Institution (1993), *Annual Report*, Instanbul (Turkey).

Islami Bank Bangladesh Limited (1993), *Annual Report*, Dhaka (Bangladesh).

Islami Bank Bangladesh Limited (1994), *Central Account Department's letter dated March 21, 1994.* Dhaka (Bangladesh).

Islamic Bank of Bahrain (1994), *Annual Report*, Manama (Bahrain).

Islamic Republic of Iran (1983), *Law of Usury-Free Banking*, Tehran (Iran).

Jordan Islamic Bank (1993), *Annual Report*, Amman (Jordan).

Kidwell, David S. and **Richard L. Peterson** (1990*)*, *Financial Institutions, Markets, and Money*, 4th Edition, Chicago (USA), The Dryden Press.

Kuwait Finance House (1977), *Guide Book Kuwait Finance House K.S.C. for Banking and Investment*, Safa (Kuwait).

Kuwait Finance House (1993), *Annual Report*, Safa (Kuwait).

Muslim Commercial Bank (1992), *Annual Report*, Karachi (Pakistan).

Presley, John (ed.) (1988), *Directory of Islamic Financial Institutions*, London (UK), Croom Helm.

Salama, Abidin A. (1990), 'Utilization of Financial Instruments: A Case Study of Faisal Islamic Bank of Sudan' in *Developing a System of Financial Instruments*, Mohamed Ariff and M.A. Mannan (eds), Jeddah (Saudi Arabia), IRTI, Islamic Development Bank.

Shallah, Ramadan (1990), 'Jordan: The Experience of the Jordan Islamic Bank' in *Islamic Financial Market*, Rodney Wilson (ed), London (UK) and New York (USA), Routledge, pp. 100-128.

The Government of Jordan (1978), *Jordan Islamic Bank for Finance and Investment Law No. 13*, Amman (Jordan).

Chapter 6
Financing Facilities

6.1 Introduction

The financing activity is one of the primary functions of Islamic banks. This activity accounts for 50 per cent to 80 per cent of the total assets of most of the Islamic banks. In fact some banks such as Islamic bank of Bahrain and Faisal Finance Institution of Turkey have allocated more than 80 per cent of their assets into financing activities. Since Islamic banks are prohibited from making loans with interest all financing operations are based on principles allowed by *Shariah*. *Shariah* has laid several financing principles. Some of these principles were prevalent during the early years of Islam and some were developed simultaneously with the emergence of Islamic banking. Among the most widely employed financing principles are *mudaraba, musharaka, murabaha, bai muazzal, ijara, ijara wa-iktina, bai-salam* and *qard hassan*.

The principles of *mudaraba* and *musharaka* are based on profit-loss sharing concepts, whereas *murabaha, bai-mua'zzal, bai salam, ijara, ijara wa-iktina* are based on mark-up. Interest free loans are given by Islamic banks under the principle of *qard hassan*. There is, however, aberration of opinions between Muslim scholars in the management of Islamic banks and about the application of these principles. While Muslim scholars are constantly suggesting that profit-loss sharing principles are the preferable principles, contemporary practice of Islamic banks seem to prefer mark-up principles. This may be because of its simplicity as well as the risk aversion of Islamic banks.

This chapter will elaborate the concept, method and scope of financing within Islam. The financing practices of various Islamic banks will also be highlighted.

6.2 The Concept, Method and Scope of Financing

Although *Shariah* has suggested three categories of principles in financing, these principles, however, fall within two concepts of financing i.e. debt creating modes of financing and non-debt creating modes of financing. In the case of debt creating modes of financing, the users of funds are obliged to repay the funds borrowed from the bank. The *Shariah* principles which fall within this category include *murabaha, bai muazzal, ijara, ijara wa-iktina, bai salam,* and *qard hassan.* On the other hand, *mudaraba* and *musharaka* (and *ijara* to some extend) are non-debt creating modes of financing. These principles which are known as investment modes of financing do not require the users to repay the total amount of funding. While debt creating modes involve a debt burden on the users, irrespective of how much they benefits from the loans, those who enjoy the investment modes are without a debt burden.

The financing methods or techniques used by Islamic banks are in accordance with the principles suggested by religious jurists. It is worth noting that besides the common principles, there are other financing methods suggested by Muslim scholars and jurists. Some of these methods, however, are either unacceptable or not widely used by Islamic banks. The Council of Islamic Ideology of Pakistan, for example, suggested methods such as the introduction of service charges for loans, indexations of advances, investment auctioning, financing on the basis of normal rate of return, and time multiple counter loans to be used by banks in line with the Islamisation of Pakistani banking system. These methods are, however, not popular amongst Islamic banks elsewhere in the world.

The kinds of financing principles and methods used by Islamic banks usually depend on the laws that govern their operations. In some cases, special laws are promulgated by the authorities. These laws indicate the principles and methods to be used by Islamic banks. In other cases these principles and methods are either in the form of directions given by the central bank or provisions in the memorandum and articles of associations. In the absence of such formal instructions or guidelines, Islamic banks use commonly accepted Islamic financing principles and methods. These methods are later verified by their own *Shariah* Supervisory Boards.

The Iranian Law for Usury Free Banking 1983, for example, describes the methods and scopes of financing facilities to be used by banks. A summary of these facilities is highlighted in Table 6.1.

Similarly for Turkey, the Communique of Undersecretariat of Treasure and Foreign Trade issued procedures relating to the utilisation of funds accumulated in the deposits facilities. Among the financing methods approved by this Communique are *murabaha*, profit and loss participation investment, and leasing (see Chapter 5 for details).

Table 6.1
Methods of Financing Operations in Iran

Types of Activity	Permissible Methods
Productive: Industrial Mining Agriculture	Instalment sales, civil partnership, legal partnership, hire purchase, forward delivery transactions, direct investment, *qard al-hasanah*, *mozaarah, mosaqat*, and *jo'alah*.
Commercial: Imports Exports Domestic	*Modarabah*, civil partnership, legal partnership, and *jo'alah*.
Services	Civil partnership, legal partnership, hire purchase, instalment sales, and *jo'alah*.
Housing: Construction Repairs	Civil partnership, hire purchase, instalment sales, qard al-hasanah, direct investment, and *jo'alah*.
Personal needs	*Qard al-hasanah*

Source: Hedayati, 1993

In countries such as Malaysia and Pakistan, the methods of financing are issued by the central banks. In Malaysia, for example, The Central Bank issued a guideline which indicates the methods to be used for various financing activities. In the case of financing acquisition of assets such as houses, buildings, vehicles and other properties, the *bai bithaman ajil* method is recommended. The principle of *ijara* is applicable for the financing of vehicles. The principle of *mudaraba* is recommended for working capital and project financing. The principle of *musharaka* is only recommended for project financing. The principle of *qard hassan* is used only for overdraft facilities and welfare loans. Similarly, the State Bank of Pakistan issued financing guidelines for various economic activities to be adopted by banks in Pakistan. These guidelines are highlighted in Table 6.2.

Table 6.1 and Table 6.2 indicate that monetary authorities in both Iran and Pakistan issued financing methods based on economic sectors. The suggestions made by the State Bank of Pakistan is, however, more specific as compared to methods of the Iranian Central Bank. The guidelines issued by monetary authorities in Malaysia and Turkey are not as comprehensive as guidelines issued by the State Bank of Pakistan. There also some differences in methods used by Islamic banks in different countries for financing particular sectors. In the case of housing, for example, there are several methods recommended by the Iranian Central Bank, but only one method available for Malaysian and Pakistani banks. While rent-sharing is recommended in Pakistan, *bai bithaman ajil* is the norm in Malaysia.

Table 6.2
Possible Modes of Financing for Various Transactions in Pakistan

Nature of Business	Basis of Financing
I. Trade and Commerce:	
a. Commodity operations of Federal and Provincial Governments and their agencies.	Mark-up in price
b. Financing of exports under the State Bank's Export Financing Scheme and the Scheme for Financing Locally Manufactured Machinery	Service charge/concessional service charge.
c. Other items of trade & commerce	*Fixed Investment:* Equity participation, P.T.Cs., leasing or hire-purchase. *Working Capital:* Profit & loss sharing or mark-up
II. Industry	*Fixed Investment:* Equity participation, P.T.Cs., modaraba certificates, leasing, hire-purchase or mark-up. *Working Capital:* Profit & loss sharing or mark-up
III. Agriculture and Fisheries:	
a. Short-term Finance	Mark-up. In the case of small fishermen who are at present eligible for interest free loans finance for the specified inputs etc. up to prescribed amount may however be waived in the case of those who repay the finance within the stipulated period and payment of the mark-up made by the State Bank to banks by debit to Federal Government Account.
b. Medium and Long-term Finance	
i. Tubewells & other wells	Leasing or hire-purchase, in addition to ownership of machinery, banks may create charge on the land in their favour as in the case of other loans to the farmers under the Passbook System.

ii. Tractors, trailers & other farm machinery and transport (including fishing boats, solar energy plants etc.).	Hire-purchase or leasing.
iii. Plough-cattle, milk cattle & other livestock.	Mark-up.
iv. Dairy & poultry.	PLS, mark-up, hire-purchase, and leasing.
v. Storage and other farm construction (viz. sheds for animals, fencing etc.).	Leasing or rent sharing basis with flexible weightage to the bank's funds.
vi. Land development.	Development charge.
vii. Orchards, including nurseries.	Mark-up, development charge or PLS basis.
viii. Forestry.	Mark-up, development charge or PLS
ix. Water course improvement.	Development charge.
IV. Housing	Rent sharing with flexible weightage to bank's funds or buy-back cum mark-up.
V. Personal Advances (other than those for business purposes and housing).	
a. Consumer durables (cars, motorcycles, scooters and household goods).	Hire-purchase.
b. For consumption purposes.	Against tangible security buy-back arrangement.

Source: Siddique, 1985 pp.158-161.

Details on methods of financing are not fully prescribed by the special Islamic banking laws of certain countries. For example, both Law No.48/1977 on the establishment of Faisal Islamic Bank of Egypt and Jordan Islamic Bank for Finance and Investment Law No.13 of 1978 do not have details on the financing methods to be used by these banks. The memorandum and articles of association of Islamic banks also seldom elaborate on details pertaining to financing methods. The common clause which appears in the memorandum and articles of all Islamic banks is the provision which states that its operations must be free from interest.

Every financing method has its own unique features. These features can be easily identified in terms of the nature of financing, the role of the capital provider in the management of funds, the level of risk bearing by the capital provider, uncertainty of rate of return, cost of capital, the relationship of the cost of capital and the rate of return on capital. The summary of these features of the most common methods of financing is given in Table 6.3.

115

Table 6.3
The Features of Islamic Financing Techniques

	Mudaraba	*Musharaka*	*Ijara*	*Bai salam*	*Murabaha*
Nature of financing	Investment based	Investment based	Leasing based	Combination of debt and trading	Combination of debt and trading
Role of the capital provider in the management of funds	Nil	Full control	Full control on the use of the finance	Nil	Full control on the use of the finance
Risk bearing by the capital provider	i) To the full extent of the capital as well as of the opportunity cost of capital. ii) For the entire period of the contract.	Same as in *mudaraba*	i) To the full extent of the capital as well as of the opportunity cost of capital. ii) Until the asset completes its life or is finally disposed of.	i) To the full extent of the capital as well as of the opportunity cost of capital. ii) Even after the expiry of the contract until the goods are finally disposed of.	i) To the full extent of the capital. ii) Only for a short period until the goods are purchased and taken over by the finance user.
Uncertainty of rate of return	Complete uncertainty	Complete uncertainty	Complete uncertainty	Complete uncertainty	Uncertainty only for a short period of the contract
Cost of capital	Uncertain ex-ante	Uncertain ex-ante	Fixed and predetermined	Uncertain ex-ante	Fixed and predetermined
Relationship of the cost of capital and the rate of return on capital	Perfect correlation	Perfect correlation	Weak correlation	No correlation	Strong correlation but not perfect

Source: Khan, 1994

As highlighted in Chapter 2 as well as Chapter 4, Islamic banks are prohibited from associating themselves with the businesses considered unlawful by *Shariah*. In most cases, however, the special Islamic banking laws do not detail the kinds of businesses prohibited by *Shariah*. For example, although the Islamic Banking Law of Malaysia does have a specific section which details the restrictions on the business of Islamic banks, these restrictions are not related to the types of businesses but is confined to the restrictions involving payment of dividends and grant of advances and loans, prohibition of loans to directors, officers and employees, and restriction of credit to a single customer. Similarly with the Islamic Banking Law of Jordan, Law No.48/1977 of the Faisal Islamic Bank of Egypt, and the Communique of Undersecretariat of Treasury and Foreign Trade of Turkey do not specify the kinds of prohibited businesses. In the case of the Usury-Free Banking Law of Iran, there are some clauses which restrict banks in Iran in their financing activities.

For example, banks in Iran are prohibited from making an investment in the production of luxury and non-essential consumer goods. Nevertheless, there is no explanation on what constitutes luxury and non-essential consumer goods. The Law also prohibits banks to enter into *mudaraba* contract with the private sector for the purpose of importation.

The Faysal Islamic Bank of Bahrain is one of the few banks which clearly outlines the businesses that the Bank cannot invest in. Section 3(a) of its memorandum of association states that in no uncertain terms that the Bank engage in trade involving alcoholic beverages, the business of borrowing and lending money at interest, the gambling industry or the pork meat industry. Surprisingly, instead of elaborating prohibited business, most memorandum and articles of associations of Islamic banks elaborate the businesses that they are allowed to participate in. The Memorandum and Articles of Association of Kuwait Finance House, for example, comprehensively details the types of businesses that the Bank is permitted to invest in. The scope of financing and investment as specified by Article 6 of the Articles of Association is listed below:

With regard to investment operations, the company may, for example:

1. Establish new companies, and participate in or provide financing to companies in existence.
2. Provide individuals, organisations and governments with studies, expertise, research, and advise on capital placements, including the provision of all services concerning such operations.
3. Open documentary credits, and provide all banking facilities with or without security, in return for participation in commercial yields.
4. Engage in various activities related to overland transport and marine and air navigation, or finance such activities for fleet construction or operation.
5. Engage in all kinds of activities related to import and export of crops and various commodities.

6. Finance trade in commodities and movables intended to be offered for sale or rent.

7. Store all kinds of commodities and crops by traditional methods or in modern cold storage facilities or installations.

8. Purchase land and other real estate either for the purpose of selling them in their original or after parcellation, or for renting them as open land including installations, buildings, and equipment added thereto.

9. Establish mutual relief associations subject to Islamic *Shariah* provisions, to insure the Company's own funds, cash deposits and all other fixed and movable assets, as well as mutual insurance organisations for the benefit of other parties.

10. Invest funds in construction activities and related engineering industries, as well as in electrical, mechanical, electronic and related activities.

11. Invest funds in activities related to metal and oil extraction, quarries, fertiliser production and other natural resources.

12. Invest funds in all agricultural enterprises related to production of natural crops, fruits and forests, or to animal husbandry or dairy or wool production.

13. Invest funds for the construction, expansion and re-planning of towns, and related infrastructure and housing.

14. Invest funds in fisheries, sponge-dredging, pearling and other marine or riverine resources.

15. Invest funds for building ships, tankers and boats of all kinds and sizes, and for construction of dry-docks, floating docks, and shipping maintenance and repair-yards.

16. Invest funds for digging, widening, dredging and maintaining canals.

17. Invest funds in public information media, such as newspaper, magazines, radio, television and cinemas, and in projects for verification, publication and dissemination of human heritage, as well as in activities related to archaeological excavations and exhibits.

In general, the Company may carry all such activities which may assist the company to realise its banking and investment objectives whether directly or through cooperation with other organisations, companies and governments, provided that it shall not do so on an usurious basis.

Although transactions with ordinary customers are on an interest-free basis, transactions between Islamic banks and government have yet to be fully Islamised. For example, the transactions between the Iranian government and banks in that country are still on a fixed rate of return basis. Similarly, the Pakistani government still maintains interest-based transactions (Ahmad, 1994). The only two banks which are actively involved in financing government activities are Bank Islam Malaysia and Kuwait Finance House. The financing activities undertaken by these two banks, however, are in the form of subscribing Islamic securities issued by the respective governments and not as direct financing. One of the reasons which prevent governments to utilise direct financing from Islamic banks is that suitable financing methods to the government sector have not been fully developed by Muslim jurists.

There are, however, a few suggestions by scholars on this subject. For example, Siddiqi (1983) suggested that loans to government under an Islamic financial system should be interest-free and provided by the public, as a result of moral suasion, possible tax breaks or mandated by law where necessary. Chapra (1985) believed that a certain portion of all private demand deposits in the banking system could be channelled to the government as a statutory interest-free loan. The third suggestion is called 'istisna' financing. The procedures involved in this method are as follows (Al Zarqa, 1992):

a. The public authority would define the specifications of the fixed investment it wants to finance, and the number of years for the repayment of the funds. Bids are invited from investors/contractors who would undertake to construct the required facilities and sell them to the public authority for a price to be paid in instalments.

b. When the facilities are built and the 'istisna' contract consummated, the full ownership of the facilities is immediately transferred to the public authority, against the deferred sales-price that would normally cover not only the construction cost but also a profit margin. That profit could legitimately (legitimately from the *Shariah* point of view) include, *inter alia*, the cost of tying up funds for the repayment period.

c. *Shariah* rules require that investors/contractors to be sellers of the constructed facilities to legitimise the return they obtain. The investors could take upon themselves the legal responsibility of getting the facilities constructed, and subcontract the work to manufacturers/contractors with the consent of the public authority. This subcontracting is not a mere formality, as it makes the investors assume the full *Shariah* responsibility of a seller, such as guaranteeing the quality and quantity of the goods sold.

d. The deferred price that the public authority will pay may be in the form of interest-free D.P.C.'s (Deferred Price Certificate of indebtedness) whose total face-value exactly equals the total deferred price. These Certificates have different maturities to match the instalment plan that has been agreed upon by the two parties. D.P.Cs represent (the public authority's) debt. *Shariah* prohibition of *riba* precludes the sale of these debt certificates which may be cashed only on a maturity and cannot have a secondary market. For the holders of such certificates (the investors in the public project) this illiquidity is a disadvantage that would have been taken into account in the deferred sales-price they agreed upon.

6.3. Financing Practices of Islamic Banks

The financing practices of Islamic banks are very similar to that of conventional banks. These practices involve the following three elements:

a. Credit appraisal
b. Documentation and disbursement
c. Supervision

6.3.1 Credit Appraisal

As explained in Chapter 2, the central objective of Islamic banks is to engage in banking businesses without interest. Although most of these banks were founded on religious foundations which require them to perform social functions, generating profits is also considered as an objective. Some banks clearly state that their financing practices are based on policies which emphasise on profitability of the proposed ventures. For example, Dar Al Maal Al Islami Trust, a pan-Islamic organisation with

25 financial subsidiaries in 15 countries clearly states that the duties in providing Islamic banking services are to be fulfilled only within economically viable conditions of profitability. Similarly, Bank Islam Malaysia's financing practices are based within the framework of viability and the capability of the proposed project to expand.

There are also cases where the financing practices are tailored in line with the bank's by-laws. In the case of Dubai Islamic Bank for example, its Articles of Association mentions the following guidelines for financing activities:

Article 62:

The Company will base all decisions related to financing applications on the economic and legal considerations and in particular:

i.   The applicant's financial capacity.
ii.   The correctness and sufficiency of the third party's financial collateral.
iii. The degree of importance and priority of the project to be financed with regard to the general interest of the Islamic nation.
iv.   Keeping the whole and proportional cost of the ideal volume of the Project within its circumstances and elements.
v.   The accurate estimates of the Project.
vi.   The economic and technical evaluation including the feasibility of the Project.
vii. The definite availability of the adequate capital required for the execution of the Project with the concerned applicant in addition to the Company's finance.
viii. The availability of the adequate administrative and technical organisation required for the Project.
ix.   The Project not being in conflict with the economic interest of the United Arab Emirates, and other Arab Islamic and friendly countries.

In view of the above explanations it is seen that the 5Cs of creditworthiness i.e. character, capacity, capital, collateral, and conditions which are widely used in the conventional banking system are also applied by Islamic banks. 'Character' involves attitude, level of knowledge in aspects of business, and the moral personality of the applicant. 'Capacity' relates to the ability to pay back the loan either from income generated by the business or from other sources. 'Capital' pertains to the amount of resources owned by the applicant prior to engaging in intended business activities. 'Collateral' refers to the properties or assets that the applicant offers to the bank as security, and 'condition' deals with the environment in which the business operates. It is important for Islamic banks to apply these factors strictly in analysing the creditworthiness of potential customers. This is because delinquency problems in Islamic banks is a serious concern. Experience has shown that *murabaha* payments are often held up, because delayed repayment is not penalised (Ariff, 1990). Contrary to popular opinion, Islamic banks do impose penalties on customers for delayed payment. This penalty, however, applies only in the event of wilful default.

6.3.2 Documentation and Disbursement

During the appraisal stage, both the bank and the customer have to agree on various terms and conditions. This includes matters such as types of financing, amount of financing, duration, repayment amount, conditions before and after disbursement, collateral to be offered to the bank, and other relevant conditions. In the case of *mudaraba* and *musharaka*, for example, both parties must agree on the profit-sharing ratio and options within the relationship. The bank has the prerogative either to become an ordinary financier or a shareholder of the customer's company. These details are normally covered in the document referred to as the 'Financing Agreement'.

Article 63 of the Articles of Association of the Dubai Islamic Bank for example, requires the following terms to be included in loan agreements:

Article 63:

All contracts between the Company (bank) and the management of the concerned projects will include all necessary conditions and explanations and in particular:

i. The financial conditions including the proportional profit of the Company as financier and the amount of money to be paid to the Company for the feasibility study, supervision or for representing the firm.

ii. The management's undertaking to provide adequate information on the progress of the concerned project, periodically from the date of signing the contract until all financial relations are settled completely.

iii. The management's undertaking to provide the Company with all required facilities to see the progress of the work for which the Company has provided finance.

iv. The details of means for ascertaining the financing of timely payments of the valid expenditure.

The Company may make direct payment for the expenditure of the authorised phases of the project.

v. The details of means which will ascertain the repayment of Company's investment and profit due. The Company may do so by direct collection of the concerned project's income.

vi. The details of means which will ascertain the accuracy of the project's accounts. The Company may do so through direct supervision of the projects accounts by the Company accountants and auditors.

vii. The details of means which will ascertain the availability of legal contracts with project personnel, contractors, subcontractors, merchants and other persons required to execute the project.

As shown above, the financing agreement between the bank and the customers is an important document which spell out the duties and responsibilities of both parties during the tenure of financing. This document will be used as the primary legal document in the event of dispute.

6.3.3 Supervision

The main objective of the supervision process is to ensure that the borrower repays both the principal and the profit component to the bank. This process begins immediately after the funds are disbursed to the customer. In the case of *mudaraba*, the customer is expected to make payment immediately after the delivery of goods, whereas for *bai muazzal*, *ijara* and *ijara wa-iktina*, payment is made by instalment on a specified due date.

Stringent supervision is expected for investment based financing such as *mudaraba*. This is largely because in *mudaraba* the bank is not entitled to participate in managing the project. Therefore, a good monitoring procedure is needed in order to prevent the customer from manipulating the accounts or other activities which may jeopardise the bank's share of profit. In the case of *musharaka*, the bank is allowed to participate in the management and decision making process, thus minimising the risk of devious manipulations.

Below is an example of procedures applied in Pakistan, for the recovery of the bank's provisional share in profits and for the adjustment of actual profit or loss when the financing activities are based on *mudaraba* or *musharaka* (Khan, 1990):

i. The company/firm would be required to give quarterly figures of its actual performance within 7 days of the close of each quarter on the pro forma on which the projections were given at the time of applying for *musharaka*. The bank will receive its share of profit at the provisional rate irrespective of the mid-term achievement of the project/venture as shown by the quarterly reports.

ii. At the end of each calendar quarter, provisional profits will be calculated and debited to *musharaka* account on the basis of daily products made up in that quarter applying the rate of provisional profit, as agreed at the time of entering *musharaka* or renewal thereof in percentage terms.

iii. The bank would stipulate a provisional rate of profit which would be the maximum limit as percentage of their funds deployed in the business. The bank would take the profit to this maximum limit, should actual profit reach or exceed this limit.

iv. If the actual profit made during the accounting year of the client is higher than the rate of provisional profit stipulated in the contract, then the remaining amount belonging to the bank would be left in the company as reserve profit to be used subsequently when there is a fall in the profit or if there is a loss.

v. In a situation where the profit is not enough and falls short of the rate of provisional profit stipulated in the contract, the entire profit would be first utilised by the bank so as to get the profit up to the provisional profit rate. The balance, if any, would be passed onto the client for appropriation.

vi. Where the bank does not get the profit up to the extent of the limit, even after applying the entire profit, the amount left in reserve, if any, would be utilised.

vii. If the bank still does not get profits up to the limit, even after utilising the total profit of the year and the amount available in the reserve, then it would have no choice but to accept whatever is available.

viii. In the case of a loss, the bank would refund the amount of provisional profit, obtained by it at the end of each quarter but would not reduce its *musharaka* amount. The loss would be allowed to remain in the books of the client. This loss would be adjusted first out of profits, if any, made in the subsequent years. In the loss year, the bank would, however, get profit up to the provisional rate of profit from the profit reserve, if any, created out their share in profit in previous years as mentioned earlier.

ix. If in the subsequent year a higher profit is made, it would first be utilised to wipe off the loss, if any, standing in the books of the client. The amount left, if any, would be utilised to provide profit to the bank up to the rate of provisional profit and, thereafter, if any amount is left, it would be utilised to compensate the bank for less profit or no profit received in the earlier years. If any amount is left after all this, it would be passed on to the client for appropriation.

x. In the case of *musharaka*, the profit and loss sharing is not for one year but for a longer span of time. Though the *musharaka* contract is renewable from year to year, at the option of the bank concerned, profit and loss sharing would continue until the bank terminates the *musharaka* agreement.

xi. On termination of *musharaka* arrangements, the profit or loss would be settled with the client as follows:

    a. First, the figures of pre-tax profit made during the years when *musharaka* arrangements were in force would be totalled up. From this figure, the total of all the loss figures, if any, made during that period would be deducted.

    b. Thereafter, the profit payable at the respective provisional rates of long-term and short-term funds obtained from banks and financial institutions, keeping in view the extent up to which these two categories of funds were utilised during the above period, would be calculated.

    c. In the case where profit made is more than that payable to the outside providers of funds calculated as per 'b' above, the remaining amount would be available to the client for appropriation.

    d. But, if the amount of profit payable to the banks and financial institutions is more than the aggregate net pre-tax profit, then the entire profit would be appropriated by the banks and financial institutions in the ratio of profits payable to each. Nothing will be given to the client.

e. When the share of profit of each bank/financial institution, determined as per 'b' or 'd' above, as the case may be, is less than the amount recovered by each or any one of these institutions during the entire period under reference on provisional basis, the excess amount received would be refunded. The shortfall, if any would be recovered from the client.

f. If the total amount of losses made during the years the *musharaka* arrangements were in force, is more than the total of the profits made during that period, the net loss would be shared between the client's own investment and long-term and short-term funds provided on a profit participation basis depending on their total utilisation during the entire period. The bank/institution would not only absorb its respective share of loss, but would also refund the provisional profit already received, if not already refunded.

xii. Since, as mentioned above, the settlement of profit and loss will be made at a future date on the termination of the *musharaka* arrangements, the bank would obtain a statement duly certified by the statutory auditors of the client, showing not only the profit and loss position but also total daily products of each of the various funds deployed in the particular year. This is necessary to avoid any subsequent dispute in this regard at the time of settlement on the termination of the *musharaka* arrangements.

Beside the above procedures there are other general conditions related to the supervision process. For example, without indicating any reason, the bank has the right to recall its investment before the expiry date. Similarly, in the case where the bank intends to dispose its share, the existing shareholders would be given the first opportunity to purchase those shares.

6.4. The Structure of Financing Facilities of Selected Islamic Banks

The financing activities of selected Islamic banks based on the principles of *Shariah* are shown in Table 6.4. Some of the general observations are listed below:

1. The five modes of financing which are commonly used by Islamic banks world-wide are *musharaka*, *mudaraba*, *murabaha*, *ijara* and *qard hassan*. However, IBB of Bahrain uses only

126

three modes of financing i.e. *musharaka, murabaha,* and *qard hassan.* Similarly, DIB of United Arab Emirates also uses three modes i.e. *musharaka, mudaraba* and *murabaha.*

2. There are some similarities among Islamic banks in adopting various principles in their financing activities. In the case of *musharaka,* for example, all Islamic banks use two types of *musharaka,* (i) permanent *musharaka,* and (ii) diminishing *musharaka.* There is no time limit for permanent *musharaka* transactions and the bank will receive an annual share of profit on a pro-rata basis. This financing technique is also referred to as continued *musharaka.* Diminishing *musharaka* is another form of *musharaka* which results in the discharging of the ownership of the asset or project by the bank. This diminishing partnership has been successfully applied by the Jordan Islamic Bank mainly to finance real estate projects.

3. Although the principles of *musharaka* and *mudaraba* are strongly recommended by Islamic scholars, hardly any Islamic bank is channelling more than ten per cent of its total financing portfolio along these modes of financing. Similarly with the principle of *qard hassan.* Except for IBBL of Bangladesh where the percentage of funds used for this mode of financing is four per cent, the percentage for other banks is less than one per cent.

4. There are some variations among Islamic banks in the use of *qard hassan* loan. The Jordan Islamic Bank Law allows the JIB to give *qard hassan* loans for productive purposes in various fields to enable the beneficiaries to start independent lives or to raise their incomes and standard of living. In case of IBB, the *qard hassan* loan is used as assistance for persons to get married, for house repairs, medical treatments and for education. At the DIB, this loan is extended for productive purposes and available to shareholders or depositors. The amount, however, is relatively small and on a short term basis. In Malaysia, *qard hassan* loans are extended by BIMB through social organisations such as Amanah Ikhtiar Malaysia or AIM (AIM is a social organisation established by the Foundation of Islamic Econom-

ics of Malaysia with the objective of increasing the income of poor Muslims).

5. The principle of *murabaha* is the most widely used principle among Islamic banks. IBB of Bahrain for example, channelled 96% of its financing activities in the form of *murabaha*. Other banks with high percentages of *murabaha* financing are 85% for DIB of United Arab Emirates, 61% for FFI of Turkey, and 51% for IBBL of Bangladesh. However, the percentage of *murabaha* for BIMB of Malaysia was less than 20%. This method is widely used by Islamic banks to satisfy different financing requirements of the sectors of the economy. There are not many variations in the usage of this principle among the Islamic banks. Basically it involves the purchase of raw materials, equipment, machinery, land and building from a third party in cash by the bank and then re-selling of these to a customer on a marked-up price agreeable by both parties i.e. the bank and the customer. The selling of goods to the customer can be on a cash or credit basis.

6. BIMB of Malaysia has the highest percentage of *bai bithaman ajil* principle of financing i.e. 68% of the total financing. Although there is no *bai bithaman ajil* principle for banks such as IBB of Bahrain, JIB of Jordan, FFI of Turkey, and DIB of United Arab Emirates, these banks incorporate a deferred payment facility within the principle of *murabaha*.

7. JIB of Jordan and FFI of Turkey have a high percentage of financing in the category of 'others' i.e. 42% for JIB and 21% for FFI. While no explanation is given by the JIB, the 'others' category for FFI comprises of short term investments abroad and advances made to vendors.

Islamic banks tend to finance all sectors within the economy. The funds however are not equally distributed amongst these sectors. The sectoral breakdown of loans is shown in Table 6.5. Since there is no standardisation among Islamic banks in classifying the distribution of financing, it creates difficulties for comparative analysis. However, some of the general conclusions drawn from the data are as follows:

Table 6.4

The Modes of Financing and Its Composition by Islamic Banks in Selected Countries

Bahrain	%	Bangladesh	%	Jordan	%	Malaysia	%	Tunisia	%	Turkey	%	UAE	%
Musharaka	4	Musharaka	3	Musharaka & Mudaraba	3	Musharaka	2	Musharaka	7	Musharaka	1	Musharaka	2
		Hire-purchase	13			Mudaraba	*					Mudaraba	2
Murabaha	96	Murabaha	51	Murabaha	44	Ijara	9	Leasing	19	Ijarah	17	Murabaha	85
		Bai mua'zzal	19	Promissory notes	11	Murabaha	18	Murabaha	54	Murabaha	61		
Qard hassan	*	Qard hassan	4	Qard hassan	*	Bai mua'zzal	68	Instalment sales	20	Qard Hassan	*		
		Others	10	Others	42	Qard hassan	*	Others	*	Others	21	Others	11
						Others	3						
Total	100	Total	100	Total	100	Total	100	Total	100	Total	100	Total	100
% of TA	88	% of TA	57	% of TA	58	% of TA	33	% of TA	68	% of TA	87	% of TA	70

Notes:

1. TA: Total assets
2. * Less than 0.5 per cent

Source: Bahrain: IBB's 1994 annual report; Bangladesh: IBBL's 1993 annual report; Jordan: JIB's 1993 annual report; Malaysia: BIMB's 1994 annual report; Tunisia: BETS's 1992 annual report; Turkey: FFI's 1993 annual report; and United Arab Emirates: DBI's 1992 annual report.

1. Sectoral financing of Islamic banks varies and is in line with the economic environment of the respective country. IBBL of Bangladesh, BMI of Iran, and FIBB of Bahrain concentrate on commercial and manufacturing sectors and the percentage was 93%, 64% and 61% respectively. Both BIMB of Malaysia and JIB of Jordan tend to concentrate on the miscellaneous sector (e.g. housing, real estate, manufacturing and services) and the percentage was 45% for BIMB and 50% for JIB. There is no sectoral concentration for FFI of Turkey.

2. Faysal Islamic Bank of Bahrain is the only bank involved in financing other banks and financial institutions. At the end of 1993, the funds allocated for this sector were 17%.

3. Except for FFI of Turkey which is heavily involved in financing the agricultural sector, other Islamic banks are not really involved in this sector. At the end of 1993, 21% of total loans of FFI went to this sector. IBBL of Bangladesh, BIMB of Malaysia and Jordan had allocated only 1%, 4% and 1% respectively, for this sector. At the end of 1992, the percentage of total loans to this sector was 7% for BMI of Iran.

6.5 Summary

The financing facilities available at Islamic banks operate on an interest-free basis and are governed by various *Shariah* principles. Among the most widely used principles are *mudaraba*, *musharaka*, *murabaha*, *bai muazzal*, *ijara*, *ijara wa-iktina*, *bai-salam* and *qard hassan*. While both *mudaraba* and *musharaka* are considered non-debt creating modes of financing, other principles are debt creating modes of financing. Unlike debt creating modes of financing, the non-debt creating modes of financing or investment modes financing do not require the users to repay the amount of funds provided by the bank.

In most cases, the application of these financing methods is in line with the guidelines issued by the respective monetary authorities. The guidelines issued by these authorities often vary from one country to another and there are cases where the situation depends entirely on the discretion of the individual bank. While Muslim scholars may suggest that profit-loss sharing modes of financing are preferable contemporary

Table 6.5

The Distribution of Financing by Sector of Islamic Banks in Selected Countries

Bahrain	%
Trading	6
Manufacturing	58
Real Estate	16
Agricultural	2
Services	1
Financial Insts.	17
Total	100

Bangladesh	%
Commercial	65
Industrial	28
Real Estate	3
Agricultural	*
Transport	2
Others	2
Total	100

Iran	%
Commerce & Services	43
Industry & Mining	18
Construction & Housing	27
Agricultural	7
Others	5
Total	100

Jordan	%
General Trade	28
Industry & Mining	9
Constructions	10
Agricultural	1
Transport	2
Miscellaneous	50
Total	100

Malaysia	%
Wholesale & Retail Trade	6
Manufacturing	24
Construction	8
Real Estate	9
Agriculture	4
Transport & Storage	1
Miscellaneous	45
Business Services	2
Others	1
Total	100

Turkey	%
Metals	21
Petro-Chem	6
Textile	13
Constructions	5
Machinery	10
Agricultural	21
Paper-Pulp	3
Food	11
Chemicals	8
Others	2
Total	100

Source: Bahrain: FIBB's 1993 annual report; Bangladesh: IBBL's 1993 annual report; Iran: BMI's 1992 annual report; Jordan: JIB's 1993 annual report; Malaysia: BIMB's 1994 annual report; Turkey: FFI's 1993 annual report.

practices of Islamic banks tends to indicate otherwise. These banks seem to prefer mark-up modes of financing.

Financing activities involve all sectors within the economy and benefit all categories of customers. The financing of the government sector however, is almost non-existent. This is largely because, Islamic banks have yet to develop financing method which is acceptable by *Shariah* and yet tailored to the needs of government. The financing facilities to corporate and commercial customers are mostly in terms of a short- and medium-term duration. The financing facility to individual customers is mostly in the form of housing loans.

Like conventional banks, the financing practices of Islamic banks are governed by normal lending criteria and involve three important elements: credit appraisal, documentation and disbursement, and supervision. A stringent financing policy is being recommended because Islamic banks are facing loan delinquency problems. The usual factors of creditworthiness: character, capacity, capital, collateral, and conditions is taken into consideration during the appraisal process. The documentation and disbursement involve procedures which safeguard the bank's interest in the case of a dispute. The reason for supervision is to ensure the bank funds are used for the intended purposes and the bank recovers both principal and profits from the investment.

With regards to the structure of financing facilities it is noted that although five modes of financing i.e. *musharaka, mudaraba, murabaha, ijara* and *qard hassan* are common throughout the world, it is *murabaha* which is the most popular. This is in view of the convenience in administering these transactions. Also the risk encountered by the bank is relatively lower in *murabaha* transactions. *Qard hassan* loans appear to be the least popular among Islamic banks. This may be because these transactions generate no monetary reward.

References and Further Reading

Ahmad, Ziauddin (1994), 'Islamic Banking: State of the Art', *Islamic Economic Studies*, Vol.2, No.1 (December), pp.1-34

Al Zarqa, Mohamed Anas (1992), '*Islamic Financing of Mute Social Infrastructure: Suggested Mode Based On Istisna* ', A paper presented at 7th Expert level Meeting of Central Banks, Monetary Authorities and Islamic Banks, Kuala Lumpur (Malaysia).

Ariff, Mohamed (1990), 'Overview on Islamic Financial Market and Instruments: Their Nature and Scope.' in *Developing A System of Financial Instruments*, Mohamed Ariff and M.A. Mannan (eds), Jeddah (Saudi Arabia), IRTI, Islamic Development Bank, pp.3-14.

Bank Islam Malaysia Berhad (1992), *Notes distributed during the seminar on Islamic Banking organised by IBBM*, Kuala Lumpur (Malaysia).

Bank Islam Malaysia Berhad, *Annual Report*, various issues.

Bank Melli of Iran (1992), *Annual Report*, Tehran (Iran).

Bank Negara Malaysia (1994), *Money and Banking in Malaysia*, Kuala Lumpur (Malaysia), Economic Dept, BNM.

Beit Ettamwill Tounsi Saudi (1992), *Annual Report*, Tunis (Tunisia).

Chapra, M. Umer (1985), *Towards a Just Monetary System*, Leicester (UK), The Islamic Foundation.

Dubai Islamic Bank (1975), *Memorandum and Articles of Association*, Dubai (U.A.E.).

Dubai Islamic Bank (1992), *Annual Report*, Dubai (U.A.E).

Dubai Islamic Bank (undated), *Information leaflet*, Dubai (U.A.E.)

El Gharb Bank of Sudan (1993), *Annual Report*, Khartoum (Sudan).

Faisal Finance Institution (1993), *Annual Report*, Istanbul (Turkey).

Faysal Islamic Bank of Bahrain (1977), *Memorandum and Articles of Association*, Manama (Bahrain).

Faysal Islamic Bank of Bahrain (1994), *Annual Report*, Manama (Bahrain).

Hedayati, S.A. Asghar (1993), *'Islamic Banking As Experienced in the Islamic Republic of Iran'*, A paper presented at International Conference on Islamic Banking, Sydney, 9-10 November.

Huq, M. Azizul (1990), 'Utilization of Financial Instruments: A Case Study of Bangladesh.' in *Developing A System of Financial Instruments*, Mohamed Ariff and M.A. Mannan (eds), Jeddah (Saudi Arabia), IRTI, Islamic Development Bank, pp.207-226.

Islamic Bank Bangladesh Limited (1994), *Central Account Department's letter dated March 21, 1994 (unpublished)*, Dhaka (Bangladesh).

Islamic Bank Bangladesh Limited (1993), *Annual Report*, Dhaka (Bangladesh).

Islamic Bank of Bahrain (1994), *Annual Report*, Manama (Bahrain).

Islamic Republic of Iran (1983), *Law of Usury-Free Banking*, Tehran (Iran).

Ismail, Abdul Halim (1992), 'Bank Islam Malaysia Berhad: Principles and Operations.' in *An Introduction to Islamic Finance*, Sheikh Ghazali et. al. (eds), Kuala Lumpur (Malaysia), Quill Publications, pp.243-283.

Ismail, Abdul Halim (1992), '*Islamic Banking in Malaysia* ', A paper presented at 7th Expert Level Meeting of Central Banks, Monetary Authorities and Islamic Banks, Kuala Lumpur (Malaysia).

Jordan Islamic Bank (1993), *Annual Report*, Amman (Jordan).

Khan, Abdul Jabbar (1990), 'Non-Interest Banking in Pakistan: A Case Study.' in *Developing A System of Financial Instruments*, Mohamed Ariff and M.A. Mannan (eds), Jeddah (Saudi Arabia), IRTI, Islamic Development Bank, pp.227-243.

Khan, M. Fahim (1994), 'Comparative Economics of Some Islamic Financing Techniques', *Islamic Economic Studies*, Vol.2, No.1 (December), pp.35-68

Kuwait Finance House (1977), *Guide Book Kuwait Finance House K.S.C. for Banking and Investment*, Safa (Kuwait).

Kuwait Finance House (1977), *Memorandum of Agreement and Articles of Association*, Safa (Kuwait).

Kuwait Finance House (1993), *Annual Report*, Safa (Kuwait).

Muslim Commercial Bank (1992), *Annual Report*, Karachi (Pakistan).

Presley, John (ed) (1988), *Directory of Islamic Financial Institutions*, London (UK), Cro om Helm.

Salama, Abidin A. (1990), 'Utilization of Financial Instruments: A Case Study of Faisal Islamic Bank of Sudan.' in *Developing A System of Financial Instruments*, Mohamed Ariff and M.A. Mannan (eds), Jeddah (Saudi Arabia), IRTI, Islamic Development Bank, pp.179-192.

Siddique, Muhammad (1985), *Islamic Banking System: Principles and Practices*, Islamabad (Pakistan), Research Associates.

Siddqi, M.N. (1983), *Banking Without Interest*, Leicester (UK), The Islamic Foundation.

The Government of Egypt (1977), *The Law No.48/1977 on the Establishment of Faisal Islamic Bank of Egypt*, Cairo (Egypt).

The Government of Jordan (1978), *Jordan Islamic Bank for Finance and Investment Law No.13*, Amman (Jordan).

The Ministry of Wakf, Egypt (1977), *Decree No.77 for 1977 Enacting the Statutes of the Faisal Islamic Bank of Egypt*, Cairo (Egypt).

Chapter 7
Other Banking Facilities

7.1 Introduction

Other facilities available at Islamic banks comprise of letters of credit, letters of guarantee, collection of bills, sale and purchase of foreign currencies, and remittance services. In most cases, facilities such as letters of guarantee, sales and purchase of foreign currencies and remittance services are provided to customers on a commission and service fee basis. There are, however, slight variations in the principles adopted by Islamic banks for letters of credit facilities.

This chapter will highlight the practices of Islamic banks in providing these facilities. The loans syndication facility which is available at selected Islamic banks will also be discussed.

7.2 International Trade

Letters of credit (L/C) and collection of trade bills facilities are available at most Islamic banks. The operational aspects of these activities are very similar to operations of conventional banks and are governed by the same International Chamber of Commerce Publication No.322. This publication seeks to standardise the operational aspects of various international financial instruments. In most cases, the letters of credit facilities are either issued based on the principle of *wakalah* or the principle of *murabaha*. In the case of *wakalah*, the customer must pay in advance the full value of the item in question prior to the issuance of the letter of credit (i.e. fully-covered L/C). In addition, the bank will receive a commission or service fee on the service rendered to customer. Under the principle of *murabaha*, however, the bank would import or purchase goods and subsequently resell to customers on a marked-up price agreeable to both parties. The title to the goods will be transferred to the customer only on the arrival of the import documents. If the customer does not have deferred payment facilities, he or she must settle in full to the bank, the resale price and other charges prior to receiving the import documents.

In Malaysia, the principle of *musharaka* is used in addition to *wakalah* and *murabaha*. In this case, the bank requires the customer to deposit a certain percentage of money (based on the agreement made with the bank) prior to the importation of goods. The bank will then issue a letter of credit and make payment using both the customer's and it's own funds. The customer is responsible for selling the goods and returning the bank's portion of capital together with a pre-determined proportion of the profit. The same approach is also adopted by Islamic banks in Bangladesh.

Islamic banks also utilise the services of banks in other countries as their agents or correspondent banks in transactions involving letters of credit. These agents or correspondent banks are normally institutions where Islamic banks have some kind of formal relationship such as their associate companies or overseas branches of banks based in countries where the Islamic bank is located. For example, the Faisal Islamic Banks of Egypt and Sudan tend to use UBAF (l'Union de Banques Arabes et Françaises) as a correspondent in London, Paris and other European centres. Likewise the United Bank of Kuwait in London is an agent for the Kuwait Finance House. Although services of these non-Islamic commercial banks are used by Islamic banks, the practice of advising, confirming, and negotiating of letters of credit are nevertheless free from *riba*. The fees relating to these services are based on commissions, thus being in line with *Shariah*.

Islamic banks also participate in schemes which are established by their respective governments to promote trade with other countries. For example, Beit Ettamwill Tounsi Saudi (BETS) of Tunisia was the agent for an Algerian banking group, for schemes which involved a line of credit of two hundred million dollars. This scheme sought to finance Algerian trade with various regions of the world, with special emphasis on trade with Tunisia. The setting up and implementation of the operations are highlighted below:

a. Exporters who wish to gain access to markets in Algeria will get advisory assistance they need at BETS Bank. The exporter negotiates his commercial contract with Algerian importer.

b. The Algerian importer requests financing for the operation from his bank. The Algerian bank then requests the financing through BETS Bank.

c. BETS Bank makes an assessment and deals with the request for financing depending on the nature of the product, the length of term and the availability of credit.

d. BETS Bank advises its requirements and financing conditions to the Algerian bank for approval according to conventional, or ad hoc conditions.

e. The Algerian importer requests his bank to open a sight irrevocable L/C to BETS Bank in favour of his exporter.

f. BETS Bank in turn confirms the letter of credit and notifies the exporter.

g. At each shipment, subsequent to the negotiation of confirming documents, BETS Bank pays cash to the exporter, retaining its commission on the confirmation and also on the payment, according to standard listed rates.

h. BETS Bank finalises the *bai murabaha* (deferred payment), or other operation documents with the Algerian bank concerned.

g. The Algerian bank then releases the documents and payment is made on a deferred basis.

i. On a specified due date, the Algerian bank will settle its account with BETS Bank and at the same time collect the outstanding liability from the importer.

The joint effort between the BETS Bank of Tunisia and Algerian banks indicates that Islamic banks are capable of handling specific financing arrangements between countries. This arrangement has paved the way for further collaboration among Islamic banks especially those who have surplus funds.

Islamic banks also provide the collection of international trade bills facilities. This service includes collection of bills for both exporters and importers. In the case where the bank is appointed as an agent for an exporter, it will send all necessary documents together with a document called the 'collection order' to its agent or correspondent bank in the buyer's country. The collection order will specify instructions such as the way in which the documents will be released and steps to be taken in the event the bill is dishonoured. When an Islamic bank acts as a collecting agent on behalf of an exporter's banker, it will also follow the instructions given in the collection order before releasing the documents to the importer/buyer. Islamic banks receive a commission for services rendered in relation to these activities.

7.3 Guarantee Facilities

Guarantee facilities refer to contracts or assurances made by Islamic bank to third parties, that its customer will fulfil his obligations towards the said third party (that is, to whom the letter of guarantee is addressed to). In this assurance the bank agrees to assume the liability of its customer in the case of default or breaching of contract as agreed between the customer and the third party. The issuance of the letter of guarantee (L/G) is usually subject to various terms and conditions. A common practice is that the bank would require the customer to cover fully or at least partially the value of the letter of guarantee. The characteristics of letters of guarantee facilities available at Bank Islam Malaysia are as follows:

a. The letter of guarantee is issued under the principle of *al-kafalah*.

b. The letter of guarantee is issued for purposes such as the successful performance of a task, the settlement of a loan, etc. Usually this guarantee may fall into the following categories:

    i) Tender guarantee;

    ii) Performance guarantee;

    iii) Guarantee for sub-contracts;

    iv) Guarantee in lieu of security deposits;

    v) Guarantee for exemption of custom duties; and

    vi) Customs bonds.

c. The bank may require the customer to place a certain amount of deposit for this facility which the bank accepts under the principle of *al-wadiah*.

d. The bank charges the customer a fee for the services it provides.

Although almost all Islamic banks tend to charge a service fee when issuing letters of guarantees, scholars believed that this practice is against the *Shariah*. Scholars argue that, this facility is merely an act of guarantee and therefore, no fee should be imposed by the bank when issuing such a letter (Ariff and Mannan, 1990). Some banks, however, do issue letters of guarantees without any service fee. The Faisal Islamic Bank of Sudan, for example, issues letters of guarantees behalf of its customers based on a profit-sharing concept. The bank is remunerated based on the percentage of profit received by customers on the transaction covered by the guarantee.

7.4 Foreign Exchange Transactions

There are two kinds of foreign exchange transactions, that is, spot and forward transactions. Spot transactions involve the immediate (officially a maximum of two working days is allowed for the exchange to take place) exchange of currency or bank deposits. Forward exchange transactions involve the exchange or delivery of currency or deposits at a specified future date. The price of one currency in terms of another is called the exchange rate. Thus, the price for spot transaction is called the spot rate and the price for a future transaction is called the forward rate.

There is no objection by Islamic jurists with regards to the spot transactions of foreign exchange. This facility is available at all Islamic banks. Forward transactions however are not available at Islamic banks in some Muslim countries. The law for Jordan Islamic Bank for example, clearly indicates that all foreign exchange transactions must be conducted on a spot basis. Similarly Islamic banks in Egypt and Sudan offer no forward transactions for foreign exchange facilities. Islamic scholars believe that the determination and movement of the forward rate is largely influenced by the rate of interest. Since interest is prohibited and there is an element of interest in this forward rate, therefore, the usage of this rate is prohibited. Furthermore, scholars believe that this dealing is more speculative rather than being regular banking operations, based on satisfying the needs of the people and serving society. Therefore, it seems appropriate for Islamic banks to avoid these transactions (Homoud, 1985).

7.5 Syndicated Loans

Islamic banks in a number of Muslim countries have started to participate in loan syndication activities. Some banks have not only become syndication members but have been selected as lead managers by borrowers. Currently the Faysal Islamic Bank of Bahrain is the leading Islamic bank in managing loan syndication facilities. At the end of 1994, this bank had successfully concluded 26 syndicated Islamic financing transactions, totalling US$2.6 billion. These transactions received participation from over fifty-six international financial institutions. The Islamic Investment Company of the Gulf (IICG) of Bahrain is also actively involved in managing syndication facilities. It latest transaction is a syndicated financing of US$23.1 million to a gas company in Pakistan. With this latest transaction, IICG has raised in excess of US$0.5 billion under its Islamic Financing Syndication Programme.

Bank Islamic Malaysia Berhad (BIMB) is the most recent Islamic bank to become the lead manager of a loan syndication facility. This bank has been appointed by the Government of Malaysia to lead and arrange a portion of the financing requirements for the new Malaysian International airport. The amount in question is estimated at RM2.2 billion (US$0.9 billion). Unlike syndication facilities arranged by Islamic banks in Bahrain where the *mudaraba* principle is followed, facilities arranged by BIMB is *bai-bithaman ajil*-based. Five financial institutions including BIMB participated in this syndication.

7.6 Other Facilities

Other banking facilities available at Islamic banks include remittance services, sale of travellers cheques, and safe deposit boxes for rental. Remittance services comprise of the transfer of money and issuing of bank drafts in local or foreign currencies. The transfer and issuing of drafts in foreign currency is based on spot transaction and a certain amount of fee is imposed on customers who use this facilitiy.

In the case of travellers cheques, Islamic banks usually become agents to travellers cheque companies to sell or to buy traveller cheques issued by those companies. Normal operational procedures involving selling and buying travellers cheques are followed by Islamic banks in these transactions. Islamic banks receive a commission based on the amount of sales and purchases of these cheques. Safe deposit box facilities are only available at selected Islamic banks. A nominal rental fee is imposed on this service.

7.7 The Structure of Other Banking Facilities of Selected Islamic Banks

The issuance of letters of credits and letters of guarantees creates contingent liabilities for Islamic banks. Similar liabilities occur when Islamic banks entered into foreign exchange contracts. The total involvements of Islamic banks in these facilities is published in the annual report under the sub-heading of 'Contingent liabilities'. Table 7.1 presents a breakdown of the 'other banking' facilities offered by selected Islamic banks. Some salient observations of Islamic banks in offering these facilities are as follows:

1. The types of additional facilities provided by Islamic banks varies from one bank to another. While letters of credit and letters of guarantee are available at all banks, facilities such as foreign exchange, bills for collection are available only in selected banks such as BMI of Iran, BIMB of Malaysia, MCB of Pakistan, IBBL of Bangladesh and KFH of Kuwait. JIB of Jordan, IBB of Bahrain, FFI of Turkey and DIB of United Arab Emirates do not provide foreign exchange contracts and bills for collection services. In the case of El Gharb of Sudan, they do provide bills for collection facilities but not foreign exchange services.

2. The degree of involvement in offering 'other banking' facilities also varies from one bank to another. FFI of Turkey, for example, has total contingent liabilities almost equivalent to total assets. Similarly, the El Gharb of Sudan has total exposure in contingent liabilities worth 89% of total assets. In contrast to FFI and El Gharb, IBB of Bahrain has the lowest exposure in terms of contingent liabilities. At the end of 1994, total contingent liabilities was only 3% of total assets for IBB. BETS of Tunisia is another bank which has a low exposure in contingent liabilities. At the end of 1992 this figure was 5% of total assets. While the corresponding percentage for BIMB of Malaysia, MCB of Pakistan and IBBL of Bangladesh was between 35% to 45%, the proportion for BMI of Iran, KFH of Kuwait, JIB of Jordan and DIB of United Arab Emirates was below 15% of total assets.

3. There are also some differences in terms of emphasis on certain facilities extended by Islamic banks to their customers. BMI of Iran, MCB of Pakistan, IBBL of Bangladesh and JIB of Jordan seem to concentrate on letters of credit facilities, whereas BIMB of Malaysia, KFH of Kuwait and DIB of United Arab Emirates tend to concentrate in providing letters of guarantee.

7.8 Summary

Facilities which relate to international trades are available at all Islamic banks. The two common facilities which are widely used by customers are letters of credit and bills sent for collections. Like conventional banks, all international trade facilities provided by Islamic banks are subject to the International Chamber of Commerce, Publication No.322. Therefore, letters of credit issued by Islamic banks could be in the form of revocable or irrevocable L/C, confirmed or unconfirmed L/C, and etc. Similar rules also apply in terms of advising, negotiating, and reimbursing the liabilities arising from these transactions.

There are three types of *Shariah* principles governing the letters of credit facilities, *wakalah*, *murabaha*, and *musharaka*. The principle of *wakalah* is employed for the fully-covered letters of credit. This principle requires the customer to deposit the full amount of the L/C value prior to the issuance of the L/C to the beneficiary. Under the principle of *mudaraba*, the bank will first import the goods and then resell them to the customers on a marked-up price agreeable to both parties. The principle of *musharaka* which is used by Islamic banks in Malaysia requires that the cost of importation (L/C value) is shared by the bank and the customer. The customer, however, is responsible to sell the goods and to return to the bank the bank's funds plus the bank's share of the profits made from this particular sale.

Guarantee facilities are also available at all Islamic banks. Like letters of credit, there are various types of letters of guarantee issued by Islamic banks. The customer may be required to deposit a certain percentage of funds (known as marginal deposit) before the bank could issue a guarantee. There are cases where the customer is required to deposit funds equivalent to the value of the guarantee.

Table 7.1
The Contingent Liabilities of Islamic Banks in Selected Countries

Bahrain	%	B'desh	%	Iran	%	Jordan	%	Kuwait	%	M'sia	%	P'tan	%	Sudan	%	Tunisia	%	Turkey	%	UAE	%
LC & LG	100	LC	90	LC	66	LC	69	LC	25	LC	13	LC	43	LC	12	CA	100	LC & LG	100	LC	40
		LG	3	LG	18	LG	28	LG	40	LG	35	LG	28	LG	7					LG	60
				IC	11			FExc	35	FExc	9	FExc	16								
		BFC	5	Others	5	Others	3			BFC	18	BFC	12	BFC	55						
		Others	2							Others	25	others	1	Others	26						
Total	100	Total	100	Total	100	Total	100	Total	100	Total	100	Total	100	Total	100	Total	100	Total	100	Total	100
% of TA	3	% of TA	38	% of TA	13	% of TA	4	% of TA	10	% of TA	36	% of TA	3	% of TA	89	% of TA	5	% of TA	99	% of TA	12

Notes:

1. LC: Letters of credit, LG: Letters of Guarantee. IC: Islamic contracts, FExc: Foreign exchange contract, BFC: Bills for collection, CA: Contra accounts, TA: Total assets.

2. Islamic contracts of Iran refer to the foreign exchange contracts facilities.

Source: Bahrain: IBB's 1994 annual report; Bangladesh: IBBL's 1993 annual report; Iran: BMI's 1992 annual report; Jordan: JIB's 1993 annual report; Kuwait: KFH's 1993 annual report; Malaysia: BIMB's 1994 annual report; Pakistan: MCB's 1993 annual report; Sudan: El Gharb's 1993 annual report; Tunisia: BETS's 1992 annual report; Turkey: FFI's 1993 annual report; United Arab Emirates: DIB's 1992 annual report.

Other types of facilities offered by Islamic banks include foreign exchange transactions, travellers cheques and remittance services. In the case of foreign exchange, transactions are based on spot and forward rates. Islamic banks in Jordan, Egypt and Sudan, however, do not deal in forward transactions. The issuance of L/Cs, L/Gs, and contracts of foreign exchange will create contingent liabilities for Islamic banks. Not all banks provide a complete range of facilities with regards to international trade. It seems that the commitment towards these facilities vary from one bank to another. For example, Islamic banks in Jordan, Bahrain, Turkey and the United Arab Emirates do not have any involvement in foreign exchange contracts and collection of bills. While the exposure of Faisal Islamic Bank of Turkey in contingent liabilities is almost equivalent to its total assets, banks in Iran, Kuwait, Jordan and the United Arab Emirates seem to have a minimal exposure.

References and Further Reading

Afzal, Tayyeb (1992), '*Faysal Islamic Bank of Bahrain: Its Operational Experience.*' A paper presented at the 7th Expert Level Meeting, Kuala Lumpur (Malaysia) 27-29 July.

Ariff, Mohammed and **M.A. Mannan** (1990), *Developing A System of Financial Instruments*, Jeddah (Saudi Arabia), IRTI, Islamic Development Bank.

Bank Islam Malaysia Berhad (1994), *Annual Report*, Kuala Lumpur (Malaysia).

Bank Meli Iran (1992), *Annual Report*, Tehran (Iran).

Beit Ettamwill of Soudi (1992), *Annual Report*, Tunis (Tunisia).

Dubai Islamic Bank (1992), *Annual Report*, Dubai (UAE).

El Gharab Bank of Sudan (1993), *Annual Report*, Khartoum (Sudan).

Faisal Finance Institution (1993), *Annual Report*, Istanbul (Turkey).

Homoud, Sami Hassan (1985), *Islamic Banking: The Adaptation of banking Practice to Conform with Islamic Law*, London (UK), Arabian Information Ltd.

Huq, M. Azizul (1990), 'Utilization of Financial Instruments: A case Study of Bangladesh.' in *Developing A System of Financial Instruments*, Mohammed

Ariff and M.A. Mannan (eds), Jeddah (Saudi Arabia), IRTI, Islamic Development Bank, pp.207-226.

Islami Bank Bangladesh Limited (1993), *Annual Report*, Dhaka (Bangladesh).

Islamic Bank of Bahrain (1994), *Annual Report*, Manama (Bahrain).

Ismail, Abdul Halim (1990), 'Sources and Uses of Funds: A case Study of Bank Islam Malaysia Berhad.' in *Developing A System of Financial Instruments*, Mohammed Ariff and M.A. Mannan (eds), Jeddah (Saudi Arabia), IRTI, Islamic Development Bank, pp.193-205.

Jordan Islamic Bank (1993), *Annual Report*, Amman (Jordan).

Khan, Abdul Jabbar (1990), 'Non-Interest Banking in Pakistan: A Case Study.' in *Developing A System of Financial Instruments*, Mohammed Ariff and M.A. Mannan (eds), Jeddah (Saudi Arabia), IRTI, Islamic Development Bank, pp.227-243.

Kuwait Finance House (1993), *Annual Report*, Safa (Kuwait).

Mohamed, Ismail H. (1990), 'Utilization of Financial Instruments: A Case Study of Egypt.' in *Developing A System of Financial Instruments*, Mohammed Ariff and M.A. Mannan (eds), Jeddah (Saudi Arabia), IRTI, Islamic Development Bank, pp.173-178.

Muslim Commercial Bank (1992), *Annual Report*, Karachi (Pakistan).

Salama, Abidin Ahmed (1990), 'Utilization of Financial Instruments: A Case Faisal Islamic Bank of Sudan.' in *Developing A System of Financial Instruments*, Mohammed Ariff and M.A. Mannan (eds), Jeddah (Saudi Arabia), IRTI, Islamic Development Bank, pp.179-192.

Chapter 8
Regulation and Monetary Policy

8.1 Introduction

As explained in Chapter 4, Islamic banks have to conform with two types of laws, *Shariah* and positive laws. While *Shariah* law is based on religious foundations, positive law is promulgated by the monetary authorities to safeguard public interest. There is no uniformity in the laws followed by Islamic banks around the world. In most Muslim countries, special laws have been passed prior to the establishment of Islamic banks and this law specifies the rules and regulations for the institution which engages in banking business based on Islamic principles. This law tends to cover Islamic banking institutions in general or particular Islamic banks which are eventually established in the country.

As an ordinary business entity, Islamic banks are bound by laws which govern normal business entities. Since Islamic banks were established as private or public limited companies, the requirements stipulated in a country's company laws apply to them. In Malaysia, for example, besides conforming to the Islamic Banking Act (1983), Bank Islam Malaysia is subject to the Malaysian Companies Act (1965). Similarly, Islamic banks in Bahrain are subject to the Bahrain Commercial Companies Law (1975), the Kuwait Finance House of Kuwait is subject to the Kuwait Commercial Companies Law (1960), and Islamic Bank Bangladesh is required to conform to provisions stipulated in the Companies Act (1913) of Bangladesh.

This chapter will highlight the regulations including by-laws that govern the operations of Islamic banks. Regulation here refers to the memorandum and articles of association, specific laws for particular Islamic banks and general laws which govern Islamic banking. This chapter also discusses intervention by the monetary authority and monetary tools employed in the Islamic banking system. The functions and duties of *Shariah* supervisory board will also be elaborated.

8.2 Memorandum and Articles of Association

As mentioned earlier, Islamic banks were incorporated as companies and these banks are either formed as private or public limited companies.

147

Generally, a private limited company is one which has (i) a limited number of membership e.g. a minimum of two and a maximum of fifty members, (ii) restrictions on the right to transfer shares, and (iii) prohibitions on public subscription of its shares.

Public limited companies, on the other hand, are generally listed on the stock exchange. Bank Islam Malaysia, for example, is a public limited company and is listed at the Kuala Lumpur Stock Exchange. Similarly, the Faysal Islamic Bank of Bahrain and Islamic banks in Egypt are listed in their respective Stock Exchanges.

Like other companies, Islamic banks have to have their own memorandum and articles of associations. The contents of these documents, however, vary from one bank to another. The memorandum of association of Dubai Islamic Bank, for example, not only embodies common clauses such as the name and founders of the company, amount of shares subscribed by founders, capital of the company, public subscription, estimated life of the company, location of the registered office of the company, objectives of the company etc., but has an additional item called 'Provision of Statute of Islam', which says:

PROVISION OF STATUTE OF ISLAM

The Company will mainly be obliged to perform all its activities and practices on the principle of 'give and take' in accordance with the Statute of Islam.

The memorandum of association of the Kuwait Finance House is known as the 'memorandum of agreement'. This document contains eleven articles. Just like Kuwait Finance House, the memorandum of association of the Faysal Islamic Bank of Bahrain also contains eleven articles. These articles include information such as the name of company, objectives of the company, location of the head office, estimated life, capital and founders of the company, and liability of the shareholders.

Articles of association of ordinary companies basically contain provisions which specify the objectives of the company, regulations on the allotment and issue of shares, call on shares, how the capital may be altered, the calling of general meetings and procedures at meetings. They also prescribe rules for the powers, duties, manner of appointment, share qualification and proceedings of directors, the secretary and company seal, how dividends are to be declared and reserves provided. In addition to these common provisions, Islamic banks usually include two extra clauses. First, the clause which prescribes that their operations are free from any element of interest, and second, a clause pertaining to the appointment of a *Shariah* Supervisory Board.

8.3 The Specific Laws

A specific law refers to legislation enacted by the authorities to govern a particular Islamic bank. In Egypt, however, two Laws were decreed by the government prior to the establishment of Faisal Islamic Bank of Egypt. First, Law No.48/1977 on the Establishment of Faisal Islamic Bank of Egypt (FIBE) in which various privileges were given to this bank and second, Decree No.77 (1977) by the Ministry of Wakf enacting the Statutes of the Faisal Islamic Bank of Egypt. Similarly, in Kuwait, Law No.72 (1977) was decreed on March 23, 1977 licensing the establishment of Kuwait Finance House (KFH). In Sudan 'The FIBS Act of the National People's Council' for Faisal Islamic Bank of Sudan was introduced in 1977. In Jordan, The Law No.13 of 1978 for Finance and Investment was decreed specially for the Jordan Islamic Bank.

Some special laws are rather brief and cursory while others are very comprehensive. The Law for KFH contains only four articles and an explanatory memorandum. These four articles mention the authorisation of the setting up of KFH, sanctioning the memorandum and articles of the company, nature of the licence, and the Ministers who sanctioned the Decree. A brief explanation about the activities of KFH is highlighted in the explanatory memorandum which states that KFH will engage in financial, insurance and various forms of investment activities without practising usury or charging interest. The Law No.48 of 1977 (FIBE), however, contains 21 articles and describes the name and objectives of FIBE, the establishment of *Shariah* Supervisory Board, share capital and other matters relating to shareholders, management of the company, and provisions pertaining to the amendment of statues.

The Law No.13 of 1978 (this law was replaced by Law No.62 of 1985) decreed for the establishment of Jordan Islamic Bank is even more detailed than the laws for KFH and FIBE. It consists 37 of Sections and can broadly be divided into eleven chapters as below:

Chapter 1: DEFINITIONS AND GENERAL PROVISIONS
(Sections 1 to 5)

Chapter 2: OBJECTS AND FUNCTIONS
(Sections 6 to 8)

Chapter 3: CAPITAL
(Sections 9 & 10)

Chapter 4: ACCEPTANCE OF DEPOSITS AND ISSUE OF
AL-MUQUARADAH BONDS
(Sections 11 to 14)

Chapter 5: RULES GOVERNING THE ACTIVITIES OF THE BANK
(Sections 15 to 24)

Chapter 6: MANAGEMENT OF THE BANK
(Section 25)

Chapter 7: GENERAL MEETINGS
(Section 26)

Chapter 8: LEGAL CONSULTANT ON ISLAMIC LAW
(Sections 27 and 28)

Chapter 9: FINAL ACCOUNTS, BALANCE SHEET, AND PROFIT
AND LOSS ACCOUNTS
(Sections 29 to 32)

Chapter 10: CHARGEABILITY TO INCOME TAX
(Section 33)

Chapter 11: GENERAL PROVISION
(Sections 34 to 37)

This goes to show how stringently some Islamic banks are guided in their activities.

8.4   The General Laws

Unlike specific laws discussed earlier, general laws cover all institutions wishing to engage in Islamic banking within a country. In short, general laws are not institution specific.

In Malaysia, for example, the Islamic Banking Act 1983 was passed by Parliament prior to the establishment of the Bank Islam Malaysia in 1983 and this law applies to all Islamic banking institutions wishing to operate in Malaysia. This law containing sixty sections, is categorised into eight parts as follows:

Part I: PRELIMINARY (Sections 1 & 2)
            (Short title, commencement, application and interpretation)

Part II: LICENSING OF ISLAMIC BANKS (Sections 3 to 13)
            (Islamic banking business to be transacted only by a licensed
            Islamic bank, Minister may vary or revoke condition of licence,
            licence not to be granted in certain cases, foreign-owned banks,
            opening of new branches, Islamic bank may establish
            correspondent banking relationship with bank outside Malaysia,
            licence fee, restriction of the use of certain words in an Islamic
            bank's name, revocation of licence, effect of revocation of
            licence, and publication of list of Islamic banks).

Part III: FINANCIAL REQUIREMENTS AND DUTIES OF ISLAMIC
            BANKS (Sections 14 to 20)
            (Maintenance of capital funds, maintenance of reserve funds,
            percentage of liquid assets, auditor and auditor's report, audited
            balance sheet, statistics to be furnished, and information of
            foreign branches).

Part IV: OWNERSHIP, CONTROL AND MANAGEMENT OF
            ISLAMIC BANKS (Sections 21 to 23)
            (Information on change in control of Islamic banks, sanction for
            reconstruction of bank required, and disqualification of directors
            and employees of banks).

Part V: RESTRICTIONS ON BUSINESS (Sections 24 to 30)
            (Restrictions on payment of dividends and grant of advances and
            loans, prohibition of loans to directors, officers and employees,
            restriction on grant of loan, advances or credit facility to
            directors, officers and employees, restriction of credit to single
            customer, disclosure of interests by directors, limitation on credit
            facility for purpose of financing the purchase or holding of
            shares, and proof of compliance to all restrictions and
            prohibitions).

Part VI: POWERS OF SUPERVISION AND CONTROL OVER
            ISLAMIC BANKS (Sections 31 to 43)
            (Investigation of banks, special investigation of banks,
            production of bank's books and documents, banking secrecy,
            action to be taken if advances are against interests of depositors,

banks unable to meet obligations to inform Central Bank, action by Central Bank if bank unable to meet obligations of conducting business to the detriment of depositors, effect of removal of office of director or appointment of a director of a bank by the Central Bank, control of Islamic bank by Central Bank, Islamic bank under control of Central Bank to co-operate with Central Bank, extension of jurisdiction to subsidiaries of banks, moratorium, and amendment of bank's constitution).

Part VII: MISCELLANEOUS (Sections 44 to 56)
(Indemnity, priority of sight and savings account liabilities, penalties on directors and managers, offences by directors, employees and agents, offences by companies and by servants and agents, prohibition on receipt of commission by staff, general penalty, power of Governor to compound, consent of the Public Prosecutor, regulations, bank holidays, application of other laws, and exemption).

Part VIII: CONSEQUENTIAL AMENDMENTS (Sections 57 to 60)
(Amendment of Banking Act 1973, amendment of Companies Act 1965, amendment of Central Bank of Malaysia Ordinance 1958, and amendment of Finance Companies Act 1969).

The above provisions are very similar to the provisions of another Malaysian law called the Banking and Financial Institution Act (1989) which regulates the banking system in Malaysia.

Similarly in Turkey, the decision to allow Islamic banks to operate was contained in Decree No.83/7506 of December 1983 and published in the Official Gazette 18256 dated December 19 1983. It contains 17 articles and deals with the method and procedures of the founding of the Special Finance House, their activities and liquidation, under the protection of the 'Exchange Value of the Turkish Currency Law Number 1567' and 'Decree Number 70 Regarding Banks'. An even more comprehensive set of rules containing 35 articles were formulated by the Undersecretariat of the Treasury and Foreign Trade and published in Official Gazette 18232 of February 25 1984.

Although both Iran and Pakistan have converted their entire banking system to the Islamic, there are little similarities in their banking laws. In Iran, following the revolution in 1979, its banking system was nationalised and the 'Law for Usury-Free Banking' was passed in parliament in August 1983. This law contains twenty-seven articles and can broadly be divided into five chapters as follows:

Chapter 1:   Objectives and duties of the banking system in the Islamic Republic of Iran
(Articles 1 & 2)

Chapter 2 :   Mobilisation of monetary resources
(Articles 3 to 6)

Chapter 3 :   Banking facilities
(Articles 7 to 17)

Chapter 4 :   Bank Markazi Jomhouri Iran and monetary policy
(Articles 18 to 20)

Chapter 5 :   Miscellaneous
(Articles 21 to 27)

As required by Section 27 of this new Law, four more notes were issued and subsequently ratified by the Islamic Consultative Assembly. These notes are considered as part of the Usury-Free Banking Law. The first note called 'Regulations Relating to the Mobilisation of Monetary Resources' contains 12 articles and was issued on December 18, 1983, the second note which was issued on January 4, 1984 consist of 76 articles called 'Regulations Relating to the Granting of Banking Facilities'. The third note comprises four articles known as 'Regulations Relating to Chapter 4 of the Law for Usury-Free Banking', whereas, the fourth note called 'Regulations Relating to Chapter 5 of the Law for Usury-Free Banking' contains 8 articles. Notes three and four were both issued on March 7. 1984. These notes illustrate the evolving process of Islamic banking in Iran.

Although Iran introduced this new law, it does not mean that previous laws which regulate the banking system are no longer operative. The provisions or articles in the Money and Banking Law of 1972 which do not violate the principles set forth in the new law nevertheless remain effective (Shojaeddini, 1993).

Unlike Iran, Pakistan does not have a single comprehensive law which deals with Islamic banks. The process of Islamisation of the whole banking system was done gradually and the rules and regulations on this matter were given on a continuing basis. The rules and regulations were usually in the form of a declaration made by the Minister of Finance or circulars issued by the State Bank of Pakistan. The first regulation was Circular No.13 dated June 20 1984 of the State Bank of Pakistan which prescribed the date of implementing the changing nature of deposit and financing facilities from interest-based to interest-free facilities. The permissible modes of financing together with the possible modes of financing for various transactions were given in this Circular. Other subsequent circulars concerning the operations of Islamic banking in Pakistan issued by the State Bank of Pakistan (the central bank for Pakistan) were Circular No.26 and No.34 dated November 26 1984 and Circular No.37 and No.38 dated December 10 1984. The only new law decreed by the Government of Pakistan immediately after Islamisation was called '*Modaraba* Companies and *Modaraba* (Flotation and Control) Ordinance, 1980'. This law, however, was not meant for the whole spectrum of Islamic banks in Pakistan but dealt specifically for the registration of *Modaraba* companies and the floating management and regulation of *Modarabas*.

8.5 Intervention by Regulatory Bodies
In the conventional banking system, there are five major goals of regulation, which are:

  a. Ensuring a safe and secure banking system
  b. Provide competition
  c. Efficient allocation of credit
  d. Customer protection
  e. Basis for monetary policy

Islamic banks, being part of the financial system, are also subject to the regulation and supervision of the monetary authorities of their respective countries. The tasks of regulating and monitoring a country's financial system are normally given to the central bank. There are many similarities in terms of powers vested to central banks of Muslim countries in regulating and supervising the Islamic banks. In Turkey, for example, besides the special decree passed by the Council of Ministers, the central bank has also issued rules governing the Islamic banks. These rules appear in Official Gazette 18348 dated March 21, 1984. In all there are 18 articles that stipulate the requirements for the application and issue of licences by the central bank. The application to operate Islamic banking in Turkey is scrutinised by the central bank and the licence is issued by the Council of Ministers based on recommendations made by the central bank. The Central Bank of Turkey is also responsible for determining the reserve and liquidity ratios, and for conducting an audit of all the accounts and operations of Islamic banks.

In Malaysia, the Islamic Banking Act 1983 prescribes the powers of the central bank on Islamic banks. Any application to establish Islamic banks in Malaysia must be forwarded to the central bank and it will appraise the application and make recommendations. The existing licence of any Islamic bank may also be revoked on the recommendation of the central bank. Islamic banks must first seek approval or report to the central bank on the following:

1. To open a new branch, agency or office in any part of Malaysia or outside Malaysia.
2. To establish corresponding banking relationship with any bank outside Malaysia.
3. A proposed change in the control of the bank.
4. Whenever a loan or advance is made and secured in the aggregate by twenty per centum or more of the paid-up capital shares of any other Islamic bank or of any licensed bank under the Banking Act 1973 incorporated in Malaysia or of any finance company licensed under the Finance Companies Act 1969.
5. To grant advances, loan and credit facilities to its directors, officers and employees.
6. In case of the inability to meet its obligations or is about to suspend payment.
7. A proposed amendment or alteration in the memorandum and articles of association.

The central bank also has the power to regulate and conduct the following tasks:

1. The maintenance of paid-up capital and the reserve funds.

2. The establishment of minimum amounts of liquid assets to be held by the bank at all times.
3. The types and contents of reports to be submitted to the Central Bank.
4. The format of presentation and contents of the financial statements prepared by Islamic banks.
5. The granting of advances, loans and credit facilities.
6. The investigation and examination on books, accounts and transactions of Islamic banks.

In Iran, however, further steps were taken by its central bank in regulating the banking system. According to Article No.20 of the Law for Usury-Free Banking, the Central Bank of Iran is empowered to intervene, and supervise, the monetary and banking activities through the following instruments:

1. Fix a minimum and/or maximum share of profit for banks in their joint venture and *mudarabah* activities; these ratios may vary for different fields of activities.
2. Designation of various fields for investment and partnership within the framework of the approved economic policies, and the fixing of a minimum prospective rate of profit for the various investment and partnership projects; the minimum prospective rate of profit may vary with respect to different branches of activities.
3. Fix minimum and maximum margins of profit, as a proportion to the cost price of the goods transacted, for banks in instalment and hire-purchase transactions.
4. Determination of types and the minimum and maximum amounts of commission for banking services (provided that do not exceed the expense of service rendered) and the fees charged for putting to use the deposits received by the banks.
5. Determination of the types, amounts, minimum and maximum bonuses subject to Article 6, and the establishment of guidelines for advertisement by banks.
6. Determination of the minimum and maximum ratio in joint venture, *mozarebeh*, investment, hire-purchase, instalment transactions, buying and selling on credit, forward deals,

mozaraah, mosaqat, jo'alah, and *gharz-al-hasaneh* for banks or any thereof with respect to various fields of activity; also fixing the maximum facility that can be granted to each customer.

It is therefore seen that in addition to laws governing the general operations of Islamic banks, the central banks are empowered to intervene in specific operative aspects of Islamic banking. These interventions are necessary since Islamic banks also play a major role in mobilising the country's funds.

8.6 Monetary Policy in Islamic Banking System

As stated earlier it is important for the central bank to maintain a sound and stable financial system. One of the ways of accomplishing this task is by introducing an effective monetary policy. The main objective of monetary policy is to establish an optimum level of money supply in the economy. The overall effectiveness of monetary policy, however, will depend on the extent of its contribution to the attainment of full employment, the prevention of high inflation and a rise in the economic growth rate. In a conventional banking system, central banks usually employ three primary methods for implementing monetary policy: open market operations, reserve requirements, and discount rate. These three methods or instruments have a similar effect on the quantity of money and credit in the economy.

Open market operations involves the purchase and sales of securities by the central bank. This is the most frequently used instrument because of its convenience and flexibility. Financial institutions are normally required to deposit funds, based on a fixed percentage of deposit liabilities at the central bank. This deposit is known as the statutory reserve deposit. Movement in the percentage of this reserve will affect the quantity of money and credit in the economy. An increase in reserve requirement's percentage reduces the quantity of money and credit in the economy and vice-versa. Loans by the central bank to financial institutions is another instrument of monetary policy. The usage of this method, however, is limited to a small number of countries. These loans are referred to as discount loans and the rate charged is normally termed as the discount rate. The central bank can also vary the discount rate in a manner designed to achieve any quantity of borrowing by financial institutions, thus affecting the amount of money and credit in the economy. If central bank wants to increase money supply and credit, it can reduce the discount rate. This lower discount rate would encourage financial institutions to increase borrowing from the discount window. Similarly, if the central bank wants to decrease money supply, a higher discount rate would deter financial institutions from additional borrowing from the central bank.

The goals of Islamic monetary policy as suggested by Chapra (1983) is presented below:

a. Economic well-being with full employment and an optimum rate of economic growth.
b. Socio-economic justice and equitable distribution of income and wealth.
c. Stability in the value of money to enable the medium of exchange to be a reliable unit of account, a just standard of deferred payments and a stable store of value.

Since open market operations and discount rates are interest-based instruments and interest is totally prohibited by *Shariah*, alternative instruments have to be introduced for the implementation of Islamic monetary policy. The Council of Islamic Ideology of Pakistan in their report on the elimination of interest from the economy, however, mentioned that most of the monetary policy instruments available to the Central Bank of Pakistan under the various banking laws of the country would remain largely unaffected in an interest-free system. The regulatory instruments that would remain wholly or largely unaffected are as follows (Ahmed, et. al., 1983):

a. Minimum cash reserve requirement
b. Liquidity ratio requirement
c. Overall ceilings on the lending and investment operations of banks
d. Mandatory targets for providing finance to priority sectors
e. Selective credit controls
f. Issue of directions to banks on various aspects of banking operations not covered by specific policy instruments
g. Moral suasion

While these instruments are being used by central banks of most Islamic countries in monitoring and supervising Islamic banks, instruments which generate results similar to open market operations and discount rates have not been fully developed in Islamic banking systems. There are other instruments suggested by Muslim scholars but these instruments are still at the theoretical level and have not been implemented by monetary authorities. Beside common instruments such as statutory reserve requirement, credit ceiling and allocation of credit to preferred sectors, Chapra (1983) suggested two additional instruments, that is, reciprocal loans and placement of current account funds at the central bank. Reciprocal loans refer to the arrangement made between the central bank and financial institutions. While loans to the central bank are on an interest-free basis, loans by the central bank to financial institutions are on a *mudaraba* basis. Financial institutions are required to place a certain percentage of total current account funds with the central bank. These funds will be used by the central bank to finance social projects. Chapra (1983), however, suggested that the central bank should pay service charges for the usage of these funds.

Khan and Mirakhor (1987) suggested that central banks should not only purchase the equities of banks and other financial institutions, but should also invest directly in the real sector of the economy on a profit sharing basis or on a joint venture basis with other banks. To finance public enterprise projects, governments of Muslim countries have been urged to issue securities or shares based on the principles of *mudaraba* (Siddiqi, 1983). Among the government of Islamic countries which have issued bonds are Malaysia and Kuwait. While bonds issued by Malaysian government were based on the principle of *qard hassan*, the principle of *mudaraba* was applied by the Central Bank of Kuwait. Other monetary instruments suggested by Muslim scholars are as follows (Ariff, 1983):

a. "Refinance ratio" which refers to the central bank's refinancing of a part of the interest-free loans provided by commercial banks.
b. "*Qard hassan*" ratio by which is meant the percentage of demand deposits that commercial banks are obliged to lend as interest-free loans.

    c. "Profit-sharing ratio" which forms the basis on which *mudaraba* investments are to take place between the banks and clients.

    d. The ratio of interest-less government securities in the investment portfolio of Islamic financial institutions.

8.7 *Shariah* Supervisory Board

Yet another regulatory body that supervises Islamic banks is called the *Shariah* supervisory committee or sometimes known as the *Shariah* supervisory board. The main function of this committee is basically to ensure that the operations of Islamic banks are not in violation of *Shariah* principles. In other words, the committee has the responsibility to ensure firstly, that banking facilities and services are in accordance to *Shariah* laws. Secondly, the investments or projects in which the bank has interests are permissible by *Shariah*, and finally the bank is managed in line with Islamic principles.

The setting up of this committee varies from country to country. In Malaysia, for example, as stipulated in Section 5 of the Islamic Banking Act, 1983, the Central Bank will not recommend the granting of a licence to Islamic banks unless it is satisfied that there is, in the articles of association of the bank concerned, provision for the establishment of a *Shariah* advisory body. The function of this body is to advise the bank on the operations of its banking business in order to ensure that they do not involve any element that is not approved by the religion of Islam. In the case of Faisal Bank of Egypt, the appointment of the *Shariah* Board is stated in Article 3 of Law No.48/1977. The Article declares that:

> "A Religious Supervisory Board shall be formed within the Bank to observe conformance of its dealings and actions with the principles and rulings of Islamic Shariah. The Bank Statues shall determine the process of forming this Board, the way it shall conduct business as well as its other functions."

The appointment of the members within the *Shariah* Board also varies from one bank to another. Article 40 of the Statutes of the Faisal Islamic Bank of Egypt, for example, states:

> "The Supervisory Board shall be composed of no more than five members selected from amongst Islamic scholars and jurists of

Comparative Law believing in the idea of the Islamic Bank. The general meeting shall appoint them every three years and shall fix their remuneration upon the proposal of the Board of Directors."

Contrary to the practice adopted by the Faisal Islamic Bank of Egypt, the appointment and dismissal of the *Shariah* Board for Faysal Islamic Bank of Bahrain is made by its Board of Directors. Article 40 of its Memorandum and Article of Association, says:

"The Board of Directors shall nominate, constitute and maintain a Religious Supervisory Board composed of at least three persons who are acknowledged experts in Islamic principles, laws and traditions. Members of the Religious Supervisory Board shall be designated by the Board of Directors and may be removed by the same at any time."

Similarly, the appointment of *Shariah* Board for Jordan Islamic Bank is made by its Board of Directors. In the case of dismissal, however, unlike Faysal Islamic Bank of Bahrain where the *Shariah* Board can be easily removed by the Board of Directors, certain procedures have to be followed by Jordan Islamic Bank. Section 27 (b) of Law No.13 of 1978 for Jordan Islamic Bank states:

"The consultant so appointed to this post may not be dismissed except on the basis of a Board resolution adopted by a two thirds majority of the members at least, and giving the grounds for such dismissal."

In countries such as Iran and Pakistan, the establishment of this committee is deemed unnecessary. This is probably because these governments have central bodies that give rulings or *'fatwas'* on banking operations. The committee's report on whether the operations of the bank are conducted according to the *Shariah* principles or otherwise are normally presented in the bank's annual report. The tasks and responsibilities of some *Shariah* boards are sometimes tailored to the objectives of the organisation at which their services are rendered to. For example, as stated in its Article 2 of the Higher Board's Statute, the *Shariah* Supervisory Board of the International Association of Islamic Banks is entrusted with the following duties (Presley, 1988):

1. To study the *'fatwa'* previously issued by the religious supervisory boards of member banks, in an attempt to make decisions identical.

2. To study the previously issued *'fatwa'* to see how far they conform with the rulings of Islamic *Shariah.*

3. To supervise the activities of Islamic banks and financial institutions and members of the Association to ensure their conformity with the rulings of the Islamic *Shariah.* In addition it has to draw the attention of the concerned parties to any potential violation of these activities. In discharging its duties, the Board has the right to go through the laws and by-laws of member banks and financial institutions and to draw their attention to whatever violation might have been made in this respect. In so doing, utmost confidentiality must be observed.

4. To issue legal religious opinions on banking and financial questions in response to requests by member Islamic banks and financial institutions, or their religious supervisory boards or the secretariat general of the Association.

5. To study matters related to financial and banking operations in response to requests for advice from Islamic financial institutions.

6. Decisions and *'fatwa'* of the Board are obligatory and binding on member banks and financial institutions in cases where these are already approved by all members. However, any member bank or financial institution is entitled to ask for reconsideration of any decision. A detailed note must then be submitted in cases of disagreement as a bank is entitled to follow any course of action in the disagreement unless it is otherwise enforced by the Board.

7. To clarify legal religious rulings on new economic questions.

8.8   Summary

There is no uniformity of law covering Islamic banks around the world. In some countries such as Iran, Malaysia and Turkey, special laws have been enacted by the governments to govern the operations of all Islamic banks in those countries. Islamic banks in countries such as Bangladesh, Bahrain, Egypt, Sudan, and The United Arab Emirates are not bound by any special law but have to conform to the ordinary laws which govern the operations of other financial institutions. There are also cases where a specific law is decreed especially for a particular Islamic bank and this law is not applicable to other Islamic bank's even though they operate in the same country. For example, Law No.48/1977 on the Establishment of Faisal Islamic Bank was decreed by the Government of Egypt prior to the formation of Faisal Islamic Bank of Egypt. Similarly, situations occurred in the case of the Faisal Islamic Bank of Sudan, Jordan Islamic Bank and Kuwait Finance House.

Islamic banks were formed as either private or public limited companies. They thus fall within the ambit of company laws of the respective countries. The shares of those banks which were established as public limited companies are traded in the stock exchange. Examples for Islamic banks traded on stock exchanges are BIMB of Malaysia, FIB of Bahrain and all Islamic banks in Egypt.

With the exception of those banks which were established under special laws, the activities and operations of other Islamic banks are guided by their memorandum and articles of associations. The memorandum of association corresponds to a statute or charter and this defines the nature of the bank. The articles of association on the other hand contain regulations for the internal administration of the bank.

Being part of the financial system, Islamic banks are subject to supervision by regulatory authorities. The task of regulating and monitoring financial systems are normally given to the central bank through various laws. Like conventional banks, Islamic banks too must conform to regulations such as deposit insurance policy, capital adequacy, disclosure requirements, liquidity, and lending policy.

Since interest-based monetary instruments such as open-market operations and discount rate are not applicable to Islamic banks, central banks have to find alternative instruments that can produce a similar impact as those of interest based instruments. Instruments such as reserve requirements, liquidity ratio requirement, minimum and maximum limits on financing operations, lending to priority sectors, and moral suasion are among the methods suggested by scholars to be used in Islamic banking systems.

Another regulatory body that supervises Islamic banks is the *Shariah* supervisory board. One of the main functions of this board is to ensure that activities of Islamic banks are free from interest. The establishment, dismissal, duties and responsibilities of this board vary from one bank to another. There are also cases where no such board exists. This is true of Iran and Pakistan. However, in these two countries the entire financial system is Islamic, so separate *Shariah* boards have been deemed to be redundant.

References and Further Reading

Ahmed, Osman (1990), 'Sudan: The Role of The Faisal Islamic Bank.' in *Islamic Financial Markets*, Rodney Wilson (ed), London (UK) & New York (USA), Routledge, pp.76-99.

Ahmed, Ziauddin, Munawar Iqbal and **M. Fahim Khan** (1983), *Money and Banking in Islam*, Jeddah & Islamabad, Institute of Policies Studies.

Ariff, Mohamed (1983), 'Comments on Monetary Policy in an Islamic Economy', in *Money and Banking in Islam*, Ziauddin Ahmed et. al (eds), Jeddah & Islamabad, Institute of Policy Studies, pp.47-52.

Aryan, Hossein (1990), 'Iran: The Impact of Islamization on the Financial System.' in *Islamic Financial Markets*, Rodney Wilson (ed), London (UK) & New York (USA), Routledge, pp.155-170.

Baldwin, David (1990), 'Turkey: Islamic Banking in a Secularist Context.' in *Islamic Financial Markets*, Rodney Wilson (ed), London (UK) & New York (USA), Routledge, pp.33-58.

Baldwin, David and **Rodney Wilson** (1988), 'Islamic Finance in Principle and Practice (with special reference to Turkey)' in *Islamic Law and Finance*, Chibli Mallat (ed), London (UK), Graham & Trotman, pp.171-189.

Basha, A and **Sami M. Khalil** (1993), '*Monetary Policy in Muslim Countries with a Dual Banking System.*' A paper presented at International Conference on Islamic Banking, Sydney (Australia).

Blair William, Austin Allison, Keith Palmer and **Peter Richards-Carpenter** (1993), *Banking and The Financial Services Act*, London, Dublin, Edinburgh, Butterworths.

Chapra, M. Umer (1983), 'Monetary Policy in an Islamic Economy', in *Money and Banking in Islam*, Ziauddin Ahmed et. al (eds), Jeddah & Islamabad, Institute of Policy Studies, pp.27-46.

Gower, L.C.B. (1992), *Gower's Principles of Modern Company Law*, 5th Edition, London, Sweet and Maxwell.

Khan, Mohsin S. and **Abbas Mirakhor** (1987), 'The Financial System and Monetary Policy in an Islamic Economy', in *Theoretical Studies in Islamic Banking and Finance*, Mohsin S. Khan & Abbas Mirakhor (eds), Texas (USA), The Institute for Research and Islamic Studies, pp.163-184

Kuwait Finance House (1977), *Memorandum of Agreement and Articles of Association*, Safa (Kuwait).

Lash, Nicholas A. (1987), *Banking Laws and Regulations*, New Jersey (USA), Prentice-Hall, Inc.

Nomani, Farhad and **Ali Rahnema** (1994), *Islamic Economic Systems*, London & New Jersey (USA), Zed Books Ltd.

Pourian, Heydar (1993), '*The Problems of a Nationalized Islamic Financial System: The Case of the Islamic Republic of Iran.*' A paper presented at International Conference on Islamic Banking, Sydney (Australia).

Presley, John R. (ed) (1988), *Directory of Islamic Financial Institutions*, London (UK), Croom Helm.

Radwan, Ahmed H. (1992), '*Alternative Tools of Supervision by Central Banks for Islamic Banks.*' A paper presented at the 7th Expert-Level Meeting on Islamic Banking, Kuala Lumpur (Malaysia).

Shallah, Ramadan (1990), 'Jordan: The Experience of the Jordan Islamic Bank..' in *Islamic Financial Markets*, Rodney Wilson (ed), London (UK) & New York (USA), Routledge, pp.100-128.

Shojaeddini, Mohammad Reza (1993), '*Instruments of Monetary Policy in Islamic Banking.*' A paper presented at International Conference on Islamic Banking, Sydney (Australia).

Siddiqi, M. Nejatullah (1983), *Banking Without Interest*, Leicester (UK), The Islamic Foundation.

The Dubai Islamic Bank (1975), *Memorandum and Articles of Association*, Dubai (The United Arab Emirates).

The Faysal Islamic Bank of Bahrain (undated), *Memorandum and Articles of Association*, Manama (Bahrain).

The Government of Dubai (1975), *Decree Regarding the Establishment of Dubai Islamic Bank*, Dubai (The United Arab Emirates).

The Government of Egypt (1977), *Decree No.77 for 1977 of Ministry of Wakf Enacting the Statutes of the Faisal Islamic Bank of Egypt*, Cairo (Egypt).

The Government of Egypt (1977), *Law No.48/1977 on the Establishment of Faisal Islamic Bank of Egypt*, Cairo (Egypt).

The Government of Jordan (1978), *Law No.13 of 1978 - Jordan Islamic Bank for Finance and Investment*, Amman (Jordan).

The Government of Malaysia (1983), *Islamic Banking Act – 1983*, Kuala Lumpur (Malaysia).

The Government of Pakistan (1980), *Modaraba Companies and Modaraba (Flotation and Control) Ordinance, 1980*, Karachi (Pakistan).

The Government of Turkey (1983), *Communique of the Undersecretariat of the Treasury and Foreign Trade – Official Gazette No 18232*, Istanbul (Turkey).

The Government of Turkey (1984), *Communique of the Central Bank of Turkey - Official Gazette 18348*, Istanbul (Turkey).

The Islamic Republic of Iran (1983), *The Law for Usury-Free Banking-1983*, Tehran (Iran).

Walker, David M. (1980), *The Oxford Companion to Law*, Oxford (UK), Clarendon Press.

Chapter 9
Islamic Financial Markets

9.1 Introduction

Overwhelming support from Muslim depositors has resulted in an unusual liquidity problem for Islamic banks. In many cases, the banks' funds remain idle because of limited investment opportunities. Islamic banks are restricted from channelling these funds to conventional financial market because most instruments are interest-based. In addition to difficulties in investing excess funds, Islamic banks also encounter obstacles to expansion. In the event of a need for growth capital, Islamic banks are not able to borrow from conventional markets, once again due to interest-based transactions.

In view of these problems, the global Islamic banking system has been contemplating on having its own financial markets. In fact some Muslim countries such as Malaysia have already started to develop a specific market for the trading of Islamic securities. The financial markets of the conventional system constitute four specific components: money markets, capital markets, mortgage markets, and future markets. The capital markets trade in instruments with an original maturity of greater than one year. The money markets deal in short-term financial instruments. Mortgage markets covers the financing of real estate. The forward and future markets involve contracts between two parties for future delivery of currencies, securities, or commodities.

Similar instruments are being developed for Islamic financial markets. However, the instruments must be without any element of interest, while at the same time accommodating the characteristics of conventional instruments. These characteristics include:

a. negotiability, that is, the ability to transfer the instrument easily from one holder to another;
b. liquidity, that is, can be easily sold when cash is required;
c. they must carry minimum risk; and
d. they must be easily valued and priced.

Since Islamic financial markets are at a developing stage, these new concepts raise many theoretical and practical questions. The objective of this chapter is to elaborate the suggestions made by Muslim scholars regarding financial instruments and also to discuss existing instruments that have been successfully developed for Islamic financial markets. An Islamic inter-bank money market developed by the Malaysian monetary authorities will also be highlighted.

9.2 Capital Markets

Capital market instruments are defined as long-term financial instruments with an original maturity exceeding one year. The purpose of these markets is to channel savings into long-term productive investments. The conventional capital markets encompass public and private long-term debt instruments and equity obligations. Examples of equity obligations are corporate stocks and examples of long-term debt instruments are government and corporate bonds.

Corporate stocks represent the owners claim on companies' assets and earnings. Stockholders are the legal owners of the company. They enjoy limited liability, which means they cannot be held personally liable for the company's debt. Simultaneously, their claim on the company's assets and earning is limited by the amount of shares owned by them. There are two main types of stocks: common and preferred. Preferred stock has characteristics of both debt and of common stock. Preferred stock differs from long-term debt in that the firm is not legally bound to pay dividend. The payment of dividends for preferred stock is usually in the form of a fixed percentage and it takes priority over common stock dividends.

The concept of 'limited liability' in the context of modern mercantile practice is conceptually new to Islam. Nowhere in the original source of Islamic *fiqh* (jurisprudence) is such practice expressly mentioned (Usmani, 1992). Muslim scholars nevertheless believe that the concept of limited liability is closely related to the concept of 'juridical person' or separate legal entity. Since *Shariah* accepts the concept of juridical person, it is therefore permissible for the Islamic banking system to deal with stocks and shares. Since stocks represent a financial claim or is a title of ownership, this certificate therefore does not constitute money. Consequently, negotiation and the transfer of ownership pertains only to the object of the certificate and not to the certificate itself which is regarded from the legal point of view as a proof of the claim. Under

Shariah, common ownership is permissible and therefore it is legal to undertake sales, pawning or donating.

In the case of preferred stock, since this instrument is associated with a pre-determined fixed rate of return, it is prohibited by *Shariah*. There are, however, suggestions that similar instrument could be introduced by using the concept of a preference dividend based on a pre-determined ratio of profit (Mannan, 1990).

The issuing of common stocks is made on the basis of *mudaraba*. Like in an ordinary public offering, a prospectus which describes the financial and non-financial aspects of the company will have to be provided to potential investors. The most important requirement of *Shariah* in the process of issuing common stocks is that investors must be aware that the contract is governed by the principle of *mudaraba*. The method of distributing returns, and the institution which will utilise the proceeds of the issued financial instruments must also be clearly stated in the contract. Another important operative aspect that is prohibited by *Shariah* is the selling of a financial instrument at a higher price (profit) during the period after it is issued and bought, but before the proceeds are invested. The transactions within this period is subject to the *Shariah* rules of disposition in money, thus, it should be sold at its face value. Therefore, the prospectus should specify as to when the stocks are permissible for transactions. Under current practice, the permissible date is usually concurrent with the date the stock is listed at the stock market. The transactions of these stocks are permitted by *Shariah* as long as the assets or financial information related to these stocks are known to buyers. The price of the listed stock is then determined by market forces.

Muslim scholars have also suggested various new instruments whose characteristics bear resemblance to government and corporate bonds. In the case of government bonds, for example, the Malaysian government has been issuing bonds called 'Government Investment Certificate' since the establishment of Islamic banking in Malaysia in 1983. These certificates are governed by the principle of *qard hassan*. Similarly, the Central Bank of Kuwait issued bonds to finance the purchase of properties held by nationals other than Gulf Co-operation Council states. Kuwait Finance House being the subscriber to these interest-free bonds was required to manage the said properties with no fee payment. This was in conformity with the regulation of the Central Bank of Kuwait. Under the terms of the Council of Ministers Resolution, Kuwait Finance House was to re-purchase the properties from the Government within a period not to exceed 10 years from December 31, 1991. There is, however, no secondary market for these bonds.

There are various types of corporate bonds in the conventional banking system, namely, mortgage bonds, debenture bonds, and subordinate debentures. Mortgage bonds typically are issued with maturities of between 20 and 40 years. They give the holder the first claim on some of, or all the issuing company's assets if default occurs. The maturity period of debenture bonds is normally up to 25 years. Unlike mortgage bonds, these bonds are not secured by assets. Subordinate debentures rank behind both mortgage bonds and debentures in their claim on the firm's assets, should default occur. Most subordinate debentures are convertible bonds. These bonds can be exchanged for common stock. However, until conversion they are corporate long-term debts, thus interest and principal payments are contractual obligations of the issuing company.

One of the widely discussed instruments to replace debenture bond is known as the 'asset-based *mudaraba*' instrument. This instrument is now widely used by Islamic banks in mobilising funds. This instrument represents monetary claim against funds under the management of Islamic bank on a fiduciary basis. The operations and arrangements of this instrument are similar to mutual fund or trust units. There are two types of asset-based *mudaraba* instruments: restricted, and unrestricted.

Unrestricted *mudaraba* is a contract where the Islamic bank (the issuing party) becomes the *mudarib* (entrepreneur) and is authorised to use full discretion in managing the affairs of the funds. The restricted *mudaraba* category on the other hand has specifications regarding period, place, purpose and type of business. Also the bank is not permited to mix its own property with the *mudaraba* assets. The bank is only allowed to perform functions that are prescribed in the prospectus or *mudaraba* agreement. From the *Shariah* point of view, the project or specified activity prescribed under restricted *mudaraba* has an independent financial liability which is separate from the liability of the *mudarib*. This is because the *mudarib* does not own this project. The role of the *mudarib* in the said project is that of a trustee who undertakes to invest other people's money. For this task the trustee receives a share of profits from the project. The trustee does not assume any risk except when losses occur due to his own negligence.

The following are the main characteristics of asset based *mudaraba* instruments (Pervez, 1996):

a. Asset valuation of the *mudaraba* is undertaken at the end of each prescribed period. A positive price movement over the previous asset-valuation date reflects return on investment which is declared on each asset valuation date. Net profit after payment of all *mudaraba* costs is distributed between the instrument holders and the bank. The bank's management fee is a fixed percentage of the profit (which is previously agreed in the *mudaraba* contract). But the bank may, on its sole discretion, reduce, but not enhance, its fee by voluntarily forgoing part thereof.

b. In the event of net loss in any valuation period, the net asset value is reduced while the bank loses its management fee for the period. The bank is responsible for loss only in the event of gross negligence or violation of the terms of the *mudaraba* contract.

c. *Mudaraba* creditors do not have any recourse to other assets of the instrument holders should their claims exceed the total assets of the *mudaraba*.

d. While for the bank's management fee being based on a fixed percentage of net profit is permitted, a fixed amount is not.

e. In line with the *mudaraba* contract, reserves, as a percentage of net profits, can be built to meet future contingencies and unforseen losses. At maturity of the *mudaraba* contract, the amount held in reserves, after meeting all cost and claims etc., are distributed to the holders of the instruments.

The move towards the introduction of the asset-based *mudaraba* instrument was first initiated by Islamic banks in Jordan. As stipulated by Law No.13 of 1978, the Jordan Islamic Bank is allowed to issue financial instruments called '*Muqaradah* bond'. This Law defined *muqaradah* bonds as "documents having a uniform value, issued by the bank in the names of the persons who subscribe thereof by paying their face value on the basis of participation by the holders of these bonds in the annual profits realised, in accordance with the terms of each separate issue of such bonds." Although the Jordan Islamic Bank was allowed to issue *muqaradah* bonds, such instruments have yet to be issued by the bank. The usage of this kind of instruments, though at limited scale was, however, undertaken by the Jordanian Government. The *Muqaradah* Bonds Act (1981) was enacted by the Jordanian Government to pave the way for the Ministry of Awkaf to develop *wakf* (mortmain) property. Among the bodies which have been allowed to issue *muqaradah* bonds in Jordan are (i) the Ministry of Awkaf, Islamic Affairs and Holy Places, (ii) public institutions with financial independence, and (iii) municipalities.

One of the most important aspects of *muqaradah* bonds, as stipulated by the *Muqaradah* Bonds Act (1981) is that the Jordanian Government guarantees the settlement of the nominal (face) value of the subscribed bonds. This guarantee is in line with the *fatwa* issued by the Jordanian *Fatwa* Committee that the Government's guarantee (government being a third party) of the value of *muqaradah* bonds is something permissible and is in accordance with the principles of *Shariah*.

Like Jordan, the Pakistani Government has also decreed a special law called the '*Modaraba* Companies and *Modaraba* (Flotation and Control) (1980)'. This Law was subsequently supplemented by the *Modaraba* Companies and *Modaraba* Rules (1981). These regulations provide the necessary framework for the flotation of *mudaraba* instruments in Pakistan. Management companies, banks and other financial institutions are permitted to register themselves as *mudaraba* companies and float a *mudaraba* for a specific or general purposes. A specific *mudaraba* is one which is set up for a particular purpose, whereas a general *mudaraba* is one which has more than one specific purpose or objective. Unlike the *muqaradah* bond in Jordan which has a maturity date, *mudaraba* instruments in Pakistan can be either for a limited period or for perpetuity.

One of the important requirements for the flotation of *mudaraba* instruments in Pakistan is that the prospectus issued by the companies which invite the public to subscribe their instruments must first be approved by the Religious Board. Besides this requirement, *mudaraba* companies as highlighted in various Sections of the *Modaraba* Compa-

172

nies and *Modaraba* (Flotation and Control) Law (1980), must observe the following conditions:

a. The *mudaraba* company shall not engage in any business of the same nature in competition with the *mudaraba* floated by it.

b. The *mudaraba* company shall subscribe in each *mudaraba* floated by it not less than 10 percent of the total amount offered for subscription.

c. The directors and officers of the *mudaraba* company or their relatives shall not obtain loans, advances or credit from *mudaraba* funds or against its security.

d. The remuneration of a *mudaraba* company shall be a fixed percentage and shall not exceed 10 per cent of net annual profits of the *mudaraba*.

e. The account of a *mudaraba* shall be audited by an auditor who is a chartered accountant within the meanings of the Chartered Accountants Ordinance, appointed by the *mudaraba* company with the approval of the Registrar. The auditor shall state in his report whether the business conducted, investments made and expenditure incurred by the *mudaraba* are in accordance with the objects, terms and conditions of the *mudaraba*.

f. Annual reports shall be circulated to *mudaraba* certificate holders within six months of the close of the accounting period. This report contains the profit and loss account, balance sheet, auditor's report and the company's report which should include business activities and the amount of profit to be distributed to the certificate holders.

This indicates that there is strict control and supervision of *mudaraba* companies in Pakistan. Based on the above requirements, it seems that *mudaraba* instruments floated in Pakistan are actually *musharaka* certificates. This is the contention of Muslim scholars based on the characteristics of the instrument. In the case where the issuer participates with his own capital, the relationship is governed by the principle of *musharaka* and not *mudaraba*. In this situation, the instrument holder and the issuer tend to be ranked equally for profits generated from the projects funded by *mudaraba* funds.

Currently, asset-based *mudaraba* instruments are available at Islamic banks in most countries especially in the form of trust units. The Islamic Development Bank being an umbrella organisation for Islamic banks worldwide, have introduced two asset-based *mudaraba* instrument schemes known as 'Islamic Banks' Portfolio' (IBP) and 'Unit Investment Fund' (UIF).

IBP is a pool of funds contributed by institutions and individual investors for the purpose of financing trade, undertaking leasing and for equity participation in corporations of Islamic countries, in accordance with the principles of *Shariah*. The scheme commenced on February, 1987. The initial subscribers were 21 Islamic banks with a total contribution of US$65 million. By the end of June, 1995 the contribution had increased to US$90 million. A key operational target was to encourage trading of IBP certificates among participants and to eventually create a secondary market conforming to *Shariah*.

The UIF was launched with an initial capital of US$100 million in 1990 and the second fund of another US$100 million was offered in January 1994. The third fund with a total of US$300 million which is being issued in several trenches was launched at the beginning of 1995. The first trench worth US$75 million was offered and fully subscribed at the launching date of this fund. The funds were used largely to finance leasing of assets and for instalment sales. The bulk of its investment portfolio are IDB related projects.

The ultimate objective of the creation of *mudaraba* instruments was to generate an efficient movement of funds endowed with negotiability and liquidity. However, the lack of a secondary market for these instruments has hampered this objective. Except for Pakistan where *mudaraba* instruments are traded at the Karachi Stock Exchange, the transactions of *mudaraba* instruments available in other countries are limited and conducted at premises of issuing institutions. Although the *mudaraba* instrument is a promising instruments within the Islamic capital market, Islamic scholars claim that such instrument may be traded in the secondary market only if at least 51% of the total assets held by the *mudaraba* are tangible assets. In the case where the amount of tangible assets is less than 51%, the instrument is categorised as a mere debt instrument thus, transaction on discount or premium is prohibited (Pervez, 1996).

A type of instrument which has some similarities with conventional mortgage bonds and subordinate debentures was recommended by the Council of Islamic Ideology and subsequently adopted by the Islamic banking Pakistan. These instruments are known as 'Participation Term Certificates'(PTCs). The salient features of these instruments are presented below (Qureshi, 1990):

a. PTCs are for a specified period not exceeding ten years excluding the grace period.

b. The broad principles governing the legal aspects of PTCs are laid down by the government by making suitable amendments in the prevailing Company Act.

c. As PTC finance is provided for a specific period, it is secured by a legal mortgage on fixed assets of the company and a floating charge on the current assets.

d. For the purpose of allocation of profit to PTC holders, the investment ranks pari-passu with equity. The sharing of profits is to be determined by mutual agreement.

e. Profits for the purpose of determining return to the PTC holders are pre-tax profits before appropriations.

f. Profits payable to PTC is a deductible expense for income tax purpose.

g. The share of PTC holders in the profit is deducted prior to the claim of shareholders in the profits of the company in any given year.

h. In case of loss, the first recourse shall be to the free reserves including the credit balance in the profit and loss accounts of the issuer and the balance of the loss will be shared between the PTC holders and other providers of funds in proportion to their funds.

i. The proceeds of the PTC are to be used exclusively for implementing the project, with the sponsors being required to give an undertaking to conduct the business with diligence and efficiency in accordance with sound engineering, financial and business practices and such other terms as may be agreed between the parties.

j. To provide protection to the purchasers of PTCs, a trustee is appointed who has the right to call for any information from the company, visit premises where the plant and machinery of the companies are located and have access to their records.

k. An option may be given to the PTC holders to convert a certain portion of outstanding PTCs into ordinary shares.

l. A rights option is given to existing ordinary stockholders to subscribe to any fresh issue of PTCs.

As indicated above, PTCs are secured by mortgage and floating charges and this feature is similar to mortgage bonds of the conventional financial system. Options given to holders to convert their certificates to ordinary shares is characteristic of subordinate debentures. Although this instrument is acceptable by Islamic banks in Pakistan, some Muslim scholars, however, doubt the permissibility of this instrument (Ariff and Mannan, 1990). This is because its legality from the *Shariah* viewpoint has yet to be established.

Another instrument suggested by Muslim scholars to be used in Islamic capital markets is an *ijara*-based instrument. When a leased payment is agreed for the full duration of the lease, the instrument will be of a fixed income type. On the other hand, if the lease agreement includes leased payments to be reviewed at certain agreed periods, the instrument will be known as floating or variable income instrument. Since this instrument represents claim of monetary value with recourse to specific assets, the sale on discount or premium is allowed by *Shariah* (Pervez, 1996).

The latest development in Islamic financial instruments has been the securitisation of debt. The debt is to finance the construction of new international airport for the Malaysian Government. This financing involved RM2.2 billion and the funds were provided by five financial institutions as primary subscribers. The transactions between government and financial institutions is being governed by the principle of *bai bithaman ajil*. These primary institutions, detach the debt securities from the notes (the promise to pay from the government to the holders) and offer to other institutions of private investors under the principle of *bai al-dayn* (debt-trading). It is worth mentioning here that the principle of *bai al-dayn* is not widely used by other Islamic banks, especially in Middle Eastern countries.

9.3 Money Markets

The most important function of the money markets is to provide an efficient means for economic units to adjust their liquidity positions. This market deals with instruments which normally possess three important characteristics namely, low default risk, short-term to maturity, and high marketability. Among the widely traded instruments in conventional money markets are treasury bills, negotiable certificate of deposits, banker's acceptances, and repurchase agreements.

Treasury bills are bills issued by Treasury and sold to investors on a discounted basis. Since these instruments pay no coupon interest, the income to the investors is the difference between the purchase price and face value of the bills. The proceeds of these bills are used to finance government operating expenditures. Treasury bills are issued with maturities of three months, six months and one year. Negotiable certificates of deposits (NCDs) are another type of time deposit facilities with a typical maturity period ranging from one to three months. A banker's acceptance is a time draft drawn on and accepted by a commercial bank. Upon acceptance, a bank will pay to the holder the face value at the maturity. A repurchase agreement consists of the sale, of a short-term security with the condition that, after a period of time the original seller will buy it back at a predetermined price.

The Islamic banking system has yet to devise a package of instruments whose characteristics are similar to those available at conventional money markets. Instruments which resemblance the banker's acceptance are however being introduced by Islamic banks in some countries. These instruments nevertheless are only available at the primary market.

One of the instruments suggested by Muslim scholars is a 'murabaha-based instrument'. This instrument is recommended due to its short-term nature and is being used by Islamic banks in facilitating trades. There are a number of convenants to be fulfilled prior to the legitimisation of the transaction. The convenants being (Pervez, 1996):

a. A seller, his agent or guardian must be the owner, through purchases, of the goods before they are sold.
b. If a buyer contracts to buy goods without making a condition of them being free of defects, it is necessary that the goods be sound and free of defects. If the goods are not of the required

description or quality, after these have been received by the buyer, without any damage occurring during custody, the buyer has the option to reject the purchase. But if the buyer contracts to buy after he has seen the goods but later finds these unsuitable, even if no change took place to the goods in the meantime, he does not have the option to rescind the purchase.

c. If goods are sold with the condition that the seller is to be free from claims from all defects, there is no option for the buyer of any defect.

d. An Islamic bank is not permitted to pass on the benefits of and recourse under manufacturer's warranty to the client. It is the manufacturer's responsible for providing services under such warranty to the client and the Islamic bank may have to act as an intermediary between the client and the manufacturer /supplier for the servicing of the warranty.

e. The seller is responsible for the goods until the purchaser has taken due possession.

f. The Islamic bank is obliged to provide a breakdown of the cost and profit and all other expenses that comprise the sale price of the goods.

g. The client only promises to purchase the goods and is not obliged to necessarily take delivery of the goods upon arrival should he have a reasonable and justifiable excuse for such refusal.

Since *murabaha*-based instruments are debt instruments, some scholars claim that trading must be at face value and discounting is not permitted. This is not the case of Islamic banker's acceptance which was widely used in Malaysia. As explained in Chapter 7, Islamic banker's acceptance facilities in Malaysia are governed by the principle of *murabaha* and *bai al-dayn*. These instruments are traded in the secondary market and discounting is permissible.

Another possible instrument for the money markets is one which is governed by the principle of *qard hassan*. This instrument represents a purely monetary claim against a client issuing the debt document. The borrower is obliged to repay only the principal amount on maturity. Most Muslim scholars believe that this instrument may be collateralised but should not carry any yield for the investor nor should it be permitted for discounting. The principle of *qard hassan* is used by the Malaysian government while issuing government investment securities. The Malaysian government also rewards the holders of these certificates (as mentioned previously, some scholars believe that if the rewards are paid regularly, then it is in conflict with *Shariah*).

9.4 Mortgage Markets

Mortgage markets refer to the markets that provide finance for real estate. There are various methods of financing available within the conventional mortgage markets. Methods such as 'standard fixed-rate mortgages', 'conditional sale agreements', 'adjustable-rate mortgage', 'balloon payment', and 'rollover and renegotiated-rate' are widely used by the providers of mortgage loans. Mortgage markets became the focus of attention when mortgage-backed securitised instruments were introduced and traded in the secondary market. These instruments can be divided into two categories, namely, pass-throughs mortgage securities and mortgage-backed bonds.

The pass-through mortgage securities refer to securities that 'pass through' all payments of principal and interest on pools of mortgages to holders of security in the pool. For example, if a person owns one per cent of a pool of securities, he is entitled to receive one per cent of all principal and interest payment made. Mortgage-backed bonds are similar to a corporate bonds which have a fixed maturity date and interest payments, except that these bonds have specific mortgages as collateral.

Mortgage markets are also available in the Islamic financial system. The providers of funds in Islamic mortgage markets are, needless to say, mainly Islamic banks. Financing methods are usually in the form of *bai muazzal* (*bai bithaman ajil* in Malaysia and *bai murabaha* in Middle Eastern countries). Secondary markets for mortgage-backed instruments have yet to be developed in the Islamic financial system. The current trend of thought of Muslim scholars is that secondary markets for these types of securities are feasible. The trading of these securities, however, must be conducted at face value. Discounting is not permitted by *Shariah* because these securities are categorised as debt instruments.

9.5   Forward and Future Markets

Forward and futures markets were designed to let people offset their price risk in future transactions which involve money, security or commodity. Both forward and future markets allow people to establish their terms of exchange prior to a future delivery date. Unlike forward markets in which the contracts are not standardised between buyer and seller, contracts in future markets are standardised. Also future contracts are made between parties involved with the transactions and the 'Futures Exchange' and not with each other.

Forward markets do exist in Islamic financial system but only on a limited scale. Future markets, however, have not been established in Islamic financial system. In the case of forward markets for money, there is divergence in opinion pertaining to the legality of such transaction from the point of view of *Shariah*. As explained in Chapter 7, Islamic banks in Jordan, Egypt and Sudan are prohibited from engaging in forward transactions, whereas both spot and forward transaction are available at Islamic banks in other countries.

Forward markets for commodities are allowed by *Shariah* under the principle of *bai salam* (an advance purchase) and *istisna* (a contract to manufacture). Therefore, there lies the possibility for the securitisation of debts that emerge from these two transactions. The legitimacy of the securitisation of debt that derives from these two instruments is not conclusive within *Shariah*. Some scholars claim that financial derivatives can be created from these transactions. Since the instruments are debt in nature, discounting is not permitted. Therefore, the transactions at secondary market must be at face value, thus, reducing its marketability. Even so, these instruments are potentially viable for secondary markets in countries where the principle of *bai al-dayn* is widely enforced. This is because in such countries these instruments are backed by trade transactions.

The most widely traded financial derivatives in forward and future markets of conventional system are warrants and options. Warrants are securities giving the holders the right to buy common stocks directly from the companies at potentially advantageous prices. These derivatives are usually issued in combination with long term debts such as bonds or debentures. Options, on the other hand, allow the holders to enter contracts to buy or sell shares, commodities, currencies or other securities at a predetermined price, called the strike price, until some future time. There are two types of options, namely, call and put. While call options give the holder the right to buy, put options give the holders the right to sell a security or a futures contract at a strike price.

The legality of warrants and options too has yet to be resolved by the *Shariah*. Some scholars believe that there is no apparent conflict between the operations of these instruments and the principles of *Shariah*. A warrant or option holder is entitled to exercise his right just as the owner of a house has the right to dispose of his property in the open market. *Shariah* also permits selling through auction or open sale to the highest bidder (Mannan, 1990). On the other hand, charging a price for an option can be considered unlawful under *Shariah* (Ariff and Mannan, 1990).

9.6   Malaysian Islamic Inter-Bank Money Market

The Malaysian Islamic inter-bank money market commenced in January 1994. This market is considered to be the first Islamic money market in the world and undertakes the following activities:

a.   Inter-bank trading in Islamic financial instruments;
b.   Islamic inter-bank investments; and
c.   Inter-bank cheque clearing system.

In order to create a feasible market, several new guidelines have been introduced by the Bank Negara Malaysia (BNM-the Central Bank of Malaysia). These include the minimum levels of profit for inter-bank investment activities and BNM acting as a lender of last resort for those using Islamic modes of financing.

9.6.1   Islamic Financial Instruments

Bank Islam Malaysia Berhad (BIMB - the only full-pledge Islamic bank in Malaysia) and other financial institutions that participate in the interest-free banking system are allowed to trade among themselves in Islamic financial instruments such as Islamic banker's acceptances. BNM has indicated that in future more Islamic financial instruments would be traded among these institutions.

9.6.2 Islamic Inter-bank Investments

Islamic inter-bank investments refer to a system whereby a participant with surplus funds can make an investment with another participant in deficit, on the basis of *mudaraba*. The features of this mechanism are:

a. The period of investment is from overnight to 12 month.
b. The minimum amount of investment is RM50,000.
c. Profit-sharing is based on the period of investment:

- for periods of one month or less, the profit-sharing ratio is 70:30 (i.e., 70 per cent for the provider of funds),
- for a period exceeding one month and up to three months, the profit-sharing ratio is 80:20, and
- for periods exceeding three months, the profit-sharing ratio is 90:10.

d. The formula for calculating the profit element to be paid to the provider of funds is:

$$X = \frac{P.r.t(k)}{36500}$$

where:

X = amount of profit (in Ringgit) to be paid to the provider of funds
P = principal investment
r = rate of profit (in % pa) before distribution for investment for one year, of the receiving bank
t = number of days invested
k = profit-sharing ratio

It is worth noting here that at present, the profit-sharing ratio is determined by BNM. Bank Negara Malaysia has indicated that in future this ratio will be based on negotiation between the participants.

9.6.3 Islamic Inter-bank Cheque Clearing System

This new clearing system was introduced by Bank Negara Malaysia for BIMB and other financial institutions that participate in the interest-free banking scheme. Cheques relating to Islamic accounts are segregated from conventional cheques for clearing purposes. All participating institutions have to maintain a clearing account with the BNM on the principle of *wadiah*. This fund is used for the settling of claims made by other banks as a result of clearing. At midnight, during automatic cheque clearing at BNM, banks having a deficit are automatically funded from the surplus of other banks on the basis of *mudaraba*. Where the surplus of other banks is insufficient to cover the deficit, additional funds are provided by BNM also on the principle of *mudaraba*. The profit ratio for this mechanism is 70:30 (i.e. 70 per cent for investor). Repayment will be made the following morning. The formula for calculating the profit is similar to the formula used in calculating profits for the Islamic interbank investments.

9.7 Summary

The role of financial markets is to bring together the providers (the buyers of financial instruments) and the users of funds (the sellers of financial instruments). In the conventional system, financial markets facilitate the process of portfolio structuring and restructuring through the creation and exchange of suitable types of financial instruments. The success of these markets depends upon the availability of alternative instruments that provide the potential suppliers of funds with an optimal combination of safety, liquidity, return and cash flow that is suitable to the investors' needs.

There are various types of financial markets in the conventional system, namely, capital markets, money markets, mortgage markets, and forward and future markets. Each individual market trades different types of instruments. Capital markets trade in instruments with an original maturity of greater than one year. The most common instruments traded in capital markets are corporate stocks and long-term government and corporate bonds. Money markets deal in short-term financial instruments such as treasury bills, negotiable certificate of deposits, banker's acceptances and repurchase agreements. Mortgage markets basically seek to finance real estate. Forward and future markets involve contracts between two parties for future delivery of currencies, financial securities, and commodities. All instruments mentioned in these four sub-markets are normally traded in two market places, that is, primary or secondary markets. The primary market refers to the transactions which involve the creation of financial securities, whereas secondary market transactions involve existing securities or securities that were initially created at primary markets.

Islamic financial markets are still at an infancy state. Financial instruments associated with interest rates are not permitted by *Shariah*. Thus, instruments such as bonds including mortgage bonds, debenture bonds, subordinate debentures, negotiable certificate of deposits, repurchase agreements are not applicable within Islamic financial markets. While the issuance of corporate stocks seem to have no contradiction with *Shariah*, conflicting views are found on the permissibility of banker's acceptances, warrants and options.

There are a few pioneering instruments which are now widely used in Islamic financial markets. These instruments are mostly in the form of asset-based *mudaraba* instruments. There are also a few other recommended instruments such as *ijara*-based instruments, *murabaha*-based instruments, *bai-salam* instruments, *istisna* instruments, and *qard hassan* instruments. While asset-based *mudaraba* and *ijara* instruments are appropriate for an Islamic capital market, *murabaha* and *qard hassan* instruments may only be suitable as instruments in money markets. Debts that arise from the transactions based on *bai-muazzal* and *bai-murabaha* are being considered as instruments in mortgage markets of certain Muslim countries. Debts that arise from *bai-salam* and *istisna* transactions seem appropriate for forwards and future markets. Some scholars argue that discounting should not be permitted for debt-backed instruments. In line with this opinion, alternative mechanisms are being considered so as to enhance the marketability of these instruments.

Malaysia is one of the pioneering countries which initiated the establishment of Islamic financial markets. In January, 1994, the Islamic inter-bank money market commenced operating in Malaysia. Inter-bank trading in Islamic financial instruments, Islamic inter-bank investments, and inter-bank cheque clearing system are the key activities of this market. The participants comprise of financial institutions which were authorised by Bank Negara Malaysia to undertake interest-free banking.

References and Further Reading

Ariff, Mohamed and **M.A. Mannan** (1990), *Developing a System of Financial Instruments*, Jeddah (Saudi Arabia), IRTI, Islamic Development Bank.

Bank Negara Malaysia (1994), *Money and Banking in Malaysia*, Kuala Lumpur (Malaysia), Economic Department, BNM.

Council of Islamic Ideology (1983), 'Elimination of Interest from the Economy' in *Money and Banking in Islam*, Ziauddin Ahmed, Munawar Iqbal and M. Fahim Khan (eds), Islamabad (Pakistan), Institute of Policy Studies, pp.103-257.

El-Hennawi, Mohamed (1990), 'Potential Islamic Certificates for Resources Mobilization.' in *Developing a System of Financial Instruments*, Mohamed Ariff and M.A. Mannan (eds), Jeddah (Saudi Arabia), IRTI, Islamic Development Bank, pp.111-128

Haron S. (1995), 'Islamic Banking: A Matter of No Interest.' *JASSA*, Vol.2 (June), pp.13-16.

Hassan, Hussein Hamed (1990), 'Financial Intermediation in the Framework of Shariah.' in *Developing a System of Financial Instruments*, Mohamed Ariff and M.A. Mannan (eds), Jeddah (Saudi Arabia), IRTI, Islamic Development Bank, pp.27-44.

Islamic Development Bank (1994), *Annual Report*, Jeddah (Saudi Arabia).

Khan, Mohsin S. and **Abbas Mirakhor** (1987), The Financial System and Monetary Policy in an Islamic Economy.' in *Theoretical Studies in Islamic Banking and Finance*, Mohsin S. Khan and Abbas Mirakhor (eds), Huston (USA), The Institute for Research and Islamic Studies, pp.163-184.

Khan, Muhammad Akram (1992), 'Commodity Exchange and Stock Exchange in an Islamic Economy.' in *An Introduction to Islamic Finance*, Sheikh Ghazali Sheikh Abod et. al. (eds), Kuala Lumpur (Malaysia), Quill Publishers, pp.314-340.

Kidwell, David S., and **Richard L. Peterson** (1990), *Financial Institutions, Markets, and Money* (4th Edition), Chicago (USA), The Dryden Press.

Mannan, M.A. (1990), 'An Appraisal of Existing Financial Instruments and Market Operations from an Islamic Perspective.' in *Developing a System of Financial Instruments*, Mohamed Ariff and M.A. Mannan (eds), Jeddah (Saudi Arabia), IRTI, Islamic Development Bank, pp.75-104.

Metwally, Mokhtar M. (1992), 'The Role of the Stock Exchange in an Islamic Economy.' in *An Introduction to Islamic Finance*, Sheikh Ghazali Sheikh Abod et. al. (eds), Kuala Lumpur (Malaysia), Quill Publishers, pp.341-351.

Pervez, Imtiaz Ahmad (1996), 'The Financial Instruments Used By Islamic Banks', *New Horizon*, No.46/47, Dec 95/Jan 96, pp.19-21.

Qureshi, D.M. (1990), 'The Role of Shariah Based Financial Instruments in A Muslim Country.' in *Developing a System of Financial Instruments*, Mohamed Ariff and M.A. Mannan (eds), Jeddah (Saudi Arabia), IRTI, Islamic Development Bank, pp.49- 67.

Usmani, Muhammad Taqi (1992), '*The Principle of Limited Liability From the Shariah Viewpoint.*' A paper presented at the 7th Expert Level Meeting of Central Banks, Monetary Authorities and Islamic Banks, Kuala Lumpur (Malaysia).

Wilson, Rodney (1994), 'Development of Islamic Financial Instruments' *Islamic Economic Studies*, Vol.2 No.1 (December), pp.103-115.

Zaman, Raquibuz (1992), 'The Operation of the Modern Financial Markets for Stocks and Bonds and Its Relevance to an Islamic Economy.' in *An Introduction to Islamic Finance*, Sheikh Ghazali Sheikh Abod et. al. (eds), Kuala Lumpur (Malaysia), Quill Publishers, pp.362-378.

Index

benevolent loan	80	credit appraisal	120-126
Bengazi	7	documentation	122-123
Bilal	54	supervision	123-126
bonds	168	credit ceiling	159
branches	71	da'if	73
Bumiputera Economic Congress	16	Dar Al-Maal Al-Islamic Trust	36
business procedures	77	dark ages	4
caliphs, righteous	2	Dawalibi	64
Canon	2	Dayn mu'ajjal	56
capability	121	debenture bonds	170
capacity	121	Decree 83/7506	24,152
capital	121	Decree No.70 Regarding Banks	152
capital markets	168-176	Decree No.77 (1977)	149
Central Bank of Kuwait	159,169	deferred payment sale	80
Central Bank of Malaysia	10,17,181	Deferred Price Certificate of	
Central Bank of Sudan	23	indebtedness	120
Central Bank of Turkey	24	demand deposit facilities	91-96,104-106,
Chapra	119,159		107
character	121	din, following	68
Christianity	2	submission	68
Christians	59	Director of Posts	64
clearing account	183	discount rate	157
collateral	121	discounting	179
commercail banks	14	Doi	71
common stocks	168,169	Dubai Islamic Bank	8,37
concept of justice	32	Dzul Hijjah	52
condemned	25	economic behaviour of muslims	38
condition	121	El Askher	12
conditional sale agreements	179	eminence	71
Connors	16	entreprenurs	42
Constituent Assembly of Pakistan	18	ethical	42
Contingent liabilities	141	European Countinent	4
contingent liabilities	143	Exchange Value of the Turkish	
conventAl banking system	45	Currency Law Number 1567	152
conventional capital markets	168	exertion	74
conventional markets	167	existence of Islamic banks	35
cost-plus financing	79	Faisal Finance Institution Incorporation	25
Council Islamic Ideology of Pakistan	78	Faisal Islamic Bank of Egypt	8,12,13
Council of Arles	2	Faisal Islamic Bank of Kibris (FIBK)	24,38
Council of Carthage	2	Faisal Islamic Bank of Sudan	8,22
Council of Elvira	2	faithful	31
Council of Islamic Ideology	7,18,158	Fakhr al-Din Razi	55
Council of Islamic Studies	5,64	fasik	74
Council of Laodicea	2	fatwas	5,64,161
Council of Ministers	24	Faysal Islamic Bank of Bahrain	36
Council of Nice	2	Federal Shariah Court	22
Councils	2	Federation of Islamic Banks	7
covenants	77	fi'l	73

Index

Index